DUH!

DUH!

The Stupid History of the Human Race

Bob Fenster

**Andrews McMeel
Publishing**

Kansas City

Duh! The Stupid History of the Human Race copyright © 2000 by Bob Fenster. All rights reserved. Printed in the United States of America. No part of this book may be used or reproduced in any manner whatsoever without written permission except in the case of reprints in the context of reviews. For information, write Andrews McMeel Publishing, an Andrews McMeel Universal company, 4520 Main Street, Kansas City, Missouri 64111.

01 02 03 04 RDC 10 9 8 7 6 5

Library of Congress Cataloging-in-Publication Data

Fenster, Bob.
    Duh! : the stupid history of the human race / Bob Fenster.
        p. cm.
    ISBN 0-7407-1002-8 (pbk.)
        1. Stupidity—History. 2. Stupidity—Anecdotes. I. Title.

BF431.F36 2000
904—dc21   00-29943

Book design by Lisa Martin
Illustrations by Matthew Taylor

--- **ATTENTION: SCHOOLS AND BUSINESSES** ---

Andrews McMeel books are available at quantity discounts with bulk purchase for educational, business, or sales promotional use. For information, please write to: Special Sales Department, Andrews McMeel Publishing, 4520 Main Street, Kansas City, Missouri 64111.

Contents

vi Contents

Acknowledgments

My biggest thanks to:

New York City for bringing me up with an early appreciation for absurdity.

My good friend Marilyn Green, a living library of curiosities, for sharing some of the gems in this book from her own collection.

My three sons—Robert Charles Conaway Bothwell, Nicholas Hammett Bothwell Fenster, and Edward Nash Bothwell Fenster—who all started laughing at an early age.

Introduction

Don't kiss a rattlesnake on the mouth.

There's one life lesson you might safely assume we don't need to be taught.

Put on the parachute *before* you jump out of the plane. Stop wasting the taxpayers' money on research to find out why convicts want to escape from prison.

We should be able to get across these low bridges of human effort without too much trouble.

Strangely enough, we seem to be a race of rattlesnake kissers.

Ever since human beings stood up on their own two legs, we've found a thousand ways to fall down again.

Luckily for us, many of them are very funny—as long as they're happening to someone else.

As a large-brained species, we talk a good game, praising our intellectual progress, the genius of our inventions, the glories of consciousness. . . . But are we the highest achievement of the life force? Or simply the most self-congratulatory race the universe has ever seen?

Let's take a look at the inverted achievements of the alternatively brained in Part 1 of this book, "The Stupid Chronicles," which exalts foolishness in all fields of human misendeavor.

Then in Part 2, "Everything You Always Wanted to Know About Stupidity but Were Too Smart to Ask," we analyze the track record of the human race as we lurch from the quest for glory to the inevitability of dumb consequences.

Part 3, "How to Destupify," offers advice from history's smartest people so we can improve our own intelligence, while the jerk next door remains as dumb as he always was.

We all make dumb mistakes. If they're dumb enough or funny enough, they may be in this book. So let's celebrate the stumbling of oafs because at any time we might find ourselves tripping in their footsteps.

Now put down that rattlesnake and enjoy yourself.

PART 1

The Stupid Chronicles

Chapter 1

Dumb Plays in the Face of Fate

Fate overwhelms intelligent strategies at every turn. Still, there are times when you can grab fate and ride the surge to triumph.

Or not. Consider:

In 1990 the University of Arizona poison control center treated a man who was bitten on the tongue while kissing a rattlesnake.

A Venezuelan farmer kept his family's hard-earned fortune, some $1,600, in a straw basket. He lost everything in 1971 when his pet goat ate the basket and everything in it.

The farmer retaliated by eating the goat. No goat ever tasted $1,600 good.

Drug-addicted comic Lenny Bruce was clowning around in a hotel room, rehearsing a routine about the difficulties a Jewish Superman would face, when he flew out the fifth-story window, broke his arm, and injured his back.

If you're a gambler, you know how rare it is to go on a prolonged winning streak. A sailor hit an incredible streak of good luck one night in 1950 at a Vegas craps table. He made twenty-seven straight passes with the dice, throwing twenty-seven winners in a row.

He could have won up to $268 million on that streak (betting the house limit with each roll). Granted, not many people would have bet that hard. But he should have won smaller but still vast amounts by any reasonable betting system.

Instead, the sailor bet so lamely that he walked away from that once-in-a-million-lifetimes streak with $750.

It's equally tough to pick winners at the racetrack. Then stupidity steps in and adds insult to insult: Every year an estimated $1 million is lost, in addition to all the other losses, by people who mistakenly throw away winning tickets.

A Japanese politician, running behind in the polls, didn't need a campaign manager, media adviser, or focus group to devise this original strategy: He faked an assassination attempt in order to gain the sympathy vote.

To make the attack look convincing, the politico stabbed himself in the leg. He severed an artery and bled to death before he could make his final campaign speech.

Sometimes fate grabs you by the collar and shouts, "Here's your golden opportunity. Make the most of it!" And we respond, "Now how can I really mess up this one?"

In 1920 the Republican Party offered Hiram Johnson a chance to run as vice president to Senator Knox of Pennsylvania. But Johnson didn't want to be vice president. He wanted to be president. He wouldn't take second position on the ticket, even though insiders told him that Knox wasn't likely to survive a full term because of a bad heart.

Fate even offered Hiram Johnson a second chance for glory. Once more, he was asked to take the vice president's slot, this time under the man who upset Knox for the nomination, Warren Harding. Again Johnson declined, saying he would take the presidency or nothing.

Both Knox and Harding, who was elected president, died within a few years. If Johnson had run as vice president with either man, he would have become president, the position he craved so much.

Instead, Calvin Coolidge, who knew how to answer when fate knocked, took Hiram Johnson's place in the White House and history.

🎲

In 1999 two Milwaukee teenagers were playing a game of fast draw with family pistols. Before starting the game, they checked the clips to make sure there were no bullets inside. They didn't check the chambers.

They drew. They shot. One boy was killed, shot through the head. The other boy took a bullet through the neck that severed his spinal column and left him paralyzed. He was then charged with murder.

A New York City boy died in 1989 while elevator surfing—riding on the top of an elevator car as it zips up and down a high-rise.

That was a dumb way to die, and it should have put an end to such a dangerous sport. Instead, other boys plunged with eyes wide open into the realm of foolish defiance of fate when they continued to elevator surf.

That year, ten more boys were crushed at the top of the elevator shaft or fell to their death off fast-plunging cars.

⊗

Boxer Gene Tunney won a controversial heavyweight championship decision in 1927. When Jack Dempsey sent him to the canvas in the seventh round, the referee saved Tunney from a knockout by giving him an extra-slow count.

Three men died from heart attacks while listening to radio reports of that strange seventh round.

The capper came from a Tunney fan who was wildly cheering for his fighter while watching round-by-round recaps posted on a news board in Los Angeles.

Was the fan dumb for cheering a fight he couldn't see? No, for not putting down the ice pick before he started jumping up and down.

The fan was rushed to the hospital after stabbing himself with the ice pick in the middle of a cheer.

⊗

Athletes can be as self-destructive as fans. Consider the baseball player who in 1889 played with shotgun shells in his pockets. While he was batting, a wild pitch plunked him in the leg and his pants exploded.

Or the hockey goalie who put a pack of matches in his uniform pocket before taking the ice in 1930. A slap shot struck the goalie's pocket, ignited the matches, and set his uniform on fire.

Billiard champion Louis Fox was playing a big money match in upstate New York in 1865 when a fly landed on his cue ball. Unable to shoo the fly away, Fox miscued, lost the game, fled the hall in shame, jumped into the river, and drowned.

In 1975 an English couple were watching their favorite TV sitcom when the man was seized by a fit of laughter that lasted for half an hour. He laughed himself right into a fatal heart attack.

Have you ever seen English sitcoms? They're not that funny.

After the funeral, his wife wrote to the show's producers, thanking them for making her husband's last moments such happy ones.

In 1982 an Arizona man drove into the desert to take some target practice. He turned his shotgun on one of the legally protected giant saguaros and pumped twice.

The blasts cut the cactus in half. It fell on the man and crushed him to death.

Bungee jumping is not a new way to defy the fates. Young boys from the South Pacific island of Vanuatu maintain a tradition of building fifty-foot towers of sticks. To prove their manhood, they climb to the top and jump off, headfirst.

The boys knot vines to their ankles. They guesstimate the vines to be slightly shorter than the distance from the top of the tower to the ground, minus their height.

Sometimes they're right.

⊛

Teenage boys in Brazil prove their courage by surfing on the top of speeding electric trains. The boys who don't squat low enough under the trestles are decapitated. Others lose their balance and grab for the wires. If they don't fall to their death, they get electrocuted.

⊛

An Arizona man out hunting in 1971 shot himself in the leg. Nothing dumb about that. Happens often enough. But to call for help, the injured man fired off his rifle—and shot himself in the other leg.

⊛

A farmer in Uruguay tried to perform self-dentistry in 1977 by shooting a painful toothache with his pistol. He managed to extract the offending tooth, but also blew out his jaw.

⊛

In 1976 a New Orleans woman sued the government to nullify the Louisiana Purchase. The court denied her suit, ruling that she was too late, since the statute of limitations had expired 167 years ago.

What's the injury rate among football players? One hundred percent. Among professional boxers, 87 percent will suffer brain damage. Careers in both professional sports are short, risky, and financially rewarding only for a small percentage of those who jump in headfirst.

Doesn't slow down the volunteer rate in either sport.

A man in Clermont, France, blew up his house with his washing machine. He told police that he was trying to remove a grease stain from a shirt by pouring a cup of gasoline in the washer. When the machine changed cycles, a spark ignited the gasoline and blew out the first floor of his home, knocking him unconscious.

"I feel a bit stupid," the man admitted later.

To offer thanks for his fiancée's healthy recovery from a life-threatening illness, a Brazilian man walked penance halfway across the country, carrying a large cross on his back.

While he was gone on this spiritual trek, his fiancée married another man.

The owner of a vegetarian health spa in Mexico insisted in his will that he be buried only in the no-smoking section of the cemetery.

Back in 1973 the Denver Broncos were nothing like the Super Bowl champs they would become more than two decades later. After a particularly bad loss, one Denver fan wrote the following suicide note: "I have been a Broncos fan since the Broncos were first organized and I can't take their fumbling anymore."

Then the fan shot himself in the head. Whatever the Broncos had was catching, because he fumbled the shot and lived.

⊕

In 1999 after the United States had been shocked by a series of shootings in which high-school students had brought guns to school to kill fellow students and teachers, a woman high-school teacher in Ohio suggested the following as a topic for a writing assignment: "If you had to assassinate one famous person who is alive right now, who would it be and how would you do it?"

In 1929 a man complaining of stomach problems required surgery. The doctors removed from his stomach buttons, nails, thimbles, salt-shaker tops, safety pins, carpet tacks, coat-rack hooks, beads, pins, and a nail file.

When the Boston Strangler was terrorizing that city in the 1960s, a Brockton woman collapsed and died of fright when a strange man knocked on her front door one day. Turned out he was an encyclopedia salesman.

⬚

A South African man shot his friend in the face while both men were taking target practice, shooting beer cans off each other's heads.

The shooter lost the contest, while the winner was seriously wounded.

Chapter 2

Dumb Moments in the Lives of Famous People

It's not that the famous are dumber than you or I. Well, maybe it is.

But when they hit those low poses, the rest of us are out there watching with a certain amount of glee. Most of *our* embarrassing moments we can keep to ourselves.

☆

In the seventeenth century, England's King Charles II collected the powdered remains from mummies of Egyptian kings. In an attempt to become as great as they were, Charles rubbed the powder all over himself.

He eventually achieved his goal, although not in the way he expected. He died just as they had.

☆

Israel's Queen Jezebel carefully put on her full makeup before committing suicide by throwing herself out a tower window. She didn't want to leave an ugly corpse.

Apparently, it didn't occur to the queen what would happen to her carefully made-up face when she hit the ground.

Movie star Warren Beatty had this bright moment of self-realization: "I'm old, I'm young. I'm intelligent, I'm stupid. My tide goes in and out."

☆

But Beatty wasn't able to match this gem of revelation from England's Princess Diana: "Brain the size of a pea, I've got."

☆

Russia's Ivan the Terrible ordered an elephant killed because it did not bow down to him.

☆

Queen Christina of Sweden had a miniature cannon built and shot tiny cannonballs at the fleas in her house.

☆

King James I of England liked to gamble at cards. He had two court attendants whose duties consisted of royal card facilitation. One of the lackeys held the cards for the king, while the other told him which cards to play.

So what exactly did the king like about playing cards?

☆

New York businessman Abe Hirschfeld made a fortune operating parking lots. He then bought the *New York Post*, but was forced to sell the paper after sixteen days when his staff published an entire issue trashing the boss.

Hirschfeld went on to start another newspaper (at a time when papers all over the country were folding). It folded within five months. He then ran for political office and lost three times, twice as a Democrat, once as a Republican.

Movie star Drew Barrymore reportedly puts dirt in her shoes before heading out to glamorous Hollywood parties. Why? So she can stay grounded.

Mao Tse-tung of China was a chain smoker (though not, one assumes, during the rigors of the Great March).

Mao defended his habit by declaring that smoking was "a form of deep-breathing exercises." He also didn't brush his green teeth or take baths.

☆

Yukio Mishima, one of Japan's greatest writers, led his militant followers to take control of a Japanese army base in 1970. He made an impassioned speech to the soldiers there, demanding a return to the noble ways of the ancient samurai.

When his pleas were scorned, Mishima committed ritual suicide, and a follower cut off his head in the samurai way.

Mishima was not alone among creative fortunates who negated the talent that made them great in the first place. Other writers and artists had difficulty remembering that you can't continue to produce great work if you're dead, and that suicide is a long-term solution to a short-term problem.

1. The master painter Vincent van Gogh shot himself to death at thirty-seven.
2. American poet Hart Crane became an alcoholic and committed suicide at thirty-two.
3. Edgar Allan Poe, one of the most original writers in American history, drank himself to death with the help of drugs.
4. The magical Welsh poet Dylan Thomas, loved and beloved around the world, drank himself to death at thirty-nine.
5. Poet Sylvia Plath committed suicide. So did the poets Thomas Chatterton, Anne Sexton, Randall Jarrell, and Robert Lowell.
6. The Russian writer Maksim Gorky shot himself in the chest but survived the botched suicide attempt.
7. Debt-ridden writer Joseph Conrad shot himself in the heart, but survived.
8. Concert pianist Arthur Rubinstein hung himself with his own belt. It broke. He survived.

☆

King Ludwig II of Bavaria spent a fortune building the fairy tale medieval castle of Neuschwanstein in non-medieval 1860.

The fortune he spent on the castle wasn't his. It belonged to the state treasury, which was one reason Ludwig was declared insane and sent to an asylum.

One of the other reasons: Ludwig invited his horse to dinner.

A king must work harder than ordinary men to achieve insanity.

☆

Movie star Humphrey Bogart, one of the smartest tough guys in film, flunked out of prep school after failing geometry, English, French, and Bible studies.

Future playwright Eugene O'Neill was kicked out of Princeton University for throwing a beer bottle through the window of the college president, who later became president of the United States—Woodrow Wilson.

Peanuts cartoonist Charles Schulz had his cartoons rejected by his high-school yearbook, then was turned down for a cartoonist's job at the Walt Disney studio.

☆

Silent movie star Charlie Chaplin, who ingratiated himself with people around the world as the persecuted little tramp, played the persecutor in his not-so-private life.

He seduced actress Lita Grey when she was sixteen and he thirty-five, after grooming her to become a starlet. When she became pregnant, he offered to pay for an abortion or give her money to marry another man. Only when threatened with statutory rape and a paternity suit did he consent to marry Lita.

During their marriage, Chaplin threatened to kill her, tried to convince her to commit suicide, and still fathered two children with her. They divorced after two years.

☆

Jazz Age writer F. Scott Fitzgerald was declared the spokesman for his rebellious generation. His first novel, *This Side of Paradise*, was a success, but his subsequent books, including the now-famous *The Great Gatsby*, were financial flops.

Yet Fitzgerald and his wife, Zelda, continued to live and spend wildly, although they no longer had the resources for it.

Fitzgerald could have found financial salvation when he was contracted to write for a movie studio. But he was so difficult for Hollywood producers to work with that the studio fired him.

He died young and in debt, while the flamboyant Zelda died in an asylum after a nervous breakdown. A classic case of great promise, squandered thoughtlessly.

☆

American poet Ezra Pound was such an intellectual master that it took other intellectuals to appreciate his mastery. Yet the acclaimed poet took sides against his own country during World War II, calling Hitler "a saint" and accusing the Jews of being evil, rather than the victims of a vast evil.

Tried for treason, Pound spent twelve years in a hospital for the criminally insane. Near the end of his life he admitted, "Everything that I touch, I spoil. I have blundered always."

This is an accurate description of the kind of monumental stupidity that only a vastly intelligent person can achieve.

☆

Convicted killer Sirhan Sirhan offered this unique plea for parole from prison: "If Robert Kennedy were alive today, he would not countenance singling me out for this kind of treatment."

Sirhan was turned down for parole and remained in prison, where he had been sentenced for assassinating Robert Kennedy.

☆

Philip III, king of Spain in the 1600s, died from a fever he contracted from sitting for too long in front of the fire.

Since he knew he was overheating, why didn't the king move away from the fire? It wasn't his royal job. The palace's fire-tending attendant, whose job it was to pull back the king's chair, was off duty.

☆

When the English poet Alexander Pope read his translation of *The Iliad*, Charles Montagu, the earl of Halifax, objected to several passages and strongly suggested that Pope rewrite them.

The poet tried to negotiate a reasonable course between the demands of poetry and those of the aristocracy: He returned to Lord Halifax a few months later, thanked him for his perceptive suggestions, and read him the corrected lines.

The earl heartily approved the changes. What the earl didn't know was that Pope had made no changes.

Writers have since used the Pope approach to rewriting on countless newspaper and magazine editors down through the years.

Newspaper magnate Joseph Pulitzer once tried to build a billboard for his *New York World* that could be seen on Mars. He abandoned the plan when he couldn't decide what language the Martians could read.

Oscar Levant, the witty radio and TV star who was also an accomplished pianist, drank forty to sixty cups of coffee a day, then complained endlessly about his insomnia.

Pulitzer Prize–winning poet John Berryman, an alcoholic, tried to kill himself by jumping off a bridge into the Mississippi River. He missed the water and landed on the riverbank.

☆

In the eighteenth century the earl of Bridgewater chose his favorite dogs to join him at table for dinner. The dogs, wearing custom-made leather boots, were draped in linen and served by butlers.

If the dogs exhibited poor table manners, the earl banished them from the table.

☆

Queen Elizabeth had needs beyond those of the average royalty. She employed one maid, whose sole job was to tend to the queen's gloves.

Elizabeth had more than two thousand pairs of gloves, which meant a typical pair could go six years without being twice tugged upon the queenly hands.

☆

France's King Louis XV spent the equivalent of $15,000 a year on coffee.

While we're brooding over java, it was the English custom in the 1600s not to put sugar or cream into coffee, but mustard. No one stepped forward to claim his share of fame for that move.

Chapter 3

Stupid Predictions

Stupidity self-promotes. Half the perceived intelligence in the world comes from people who learned to keep their big mouths shut.

Consider the following people who didn't:

Charles Duell, commissioner of the U.S. Office of Patents, in 1899: "Everything that can be invented has been invented."

Oxford professor Erasmus Wilson: "When the Paris Exhibition [of 1878] closes, electric light will close with it and no more will be heard of it."

The *Literary Digest* in 1899: "[The automobile] will never, of course, come into as common use as the bicycle."

Professional well drillers when Edwin Drake tried to convince them to help him drill for oil in 1859: "Drill for oil? You mean drill into the ground to try and find oil? You're crazy."

A Western Union executive rejecting a new technology in 1876: "This 'telephone' has too many shortcomings to be seriously considered as a means of communication. The device is inherently of no value to us."

✇

An editorial in a Boston newspaper in 1865: "Well-informed people know it is impossible to transmit the voice over wires and that were it possible to do so, the thing would be of no practical value."

✇

French physiology professor Pierre Pachet in 1872: "[Louis Pasteur's] theory of germs is a ridiculous fiction."

✇

Lord Kelvin, president of England's Royal Society in 1895: "Heavier-than-air flying machines are impossible."

✇

An American newspaper editor suggesting in 1889 that the great British writer should find another trade: "I'm sorry, Mr. Kipling, but you just don't know how to use the English language."

✇

Sir John Eric Ericksen, British surgeon to Queen Victoria in 1873: "The abdomen, the chest, and the brain will forever be shut from the intrusion of the wise and humane surgeon."

Marshal Ferdinand Foch, professor of military strategy at France's École Superieure de Guerre, in the days before World War I: "Airplanes are interesting toys, but of no military value."

🔮

H. M. Warner, head of Warner Bros. studio, rejecting a new movie technology in 1927: "Who the hell wants to hear actors talk?"

🔮

A business partner of radio pioneer David Sarnoff explaining in the 1920s why they should not go into the radio business, as Sarnoff suggested: "The wireless music box has no imaginable commercial value. Who would pay for a message sent to nobody in particular?"

Yale economist Irving Fischer, a week before the 1929 stock market crash that led to the Great Depression: "Stocks have reached what looks like a permanently high plateau."

Engineer Lee DeForest in 1926: "While theoretically and technically television may be feasible, commercially and financially I consider it an impossibility."

Newspaper columnist Dorothy Thompson upon visiting Germany in 1931: "When finally I walked into Adolf Hitler's salon in the Kaiserhof Hotel, I was convinced that I was meeting the future dictator of Germany. In something less than fifty seconds I was quite sure I was not."

☺

The *Daily Express*, a British newspaper: "Britain will not be involved in a European war this year [1938], or next year either."

☺

Movie studio boss Irving Thalberg explaining why he didn't want to make *Gone with the Wind*: "No Civil War picture has ever made a nickel."

☺

Actor Gary Cooper on his decision to reject the lead role in *Gone with the Wind*: "I'm just glad it'll be Clark Gable who's falling on his face and not Gary Cooper."

☺

Thomas Watson, IBM chairman, evaluating the business potential of a new contraption in 1943: "I think there is a world market for maybe five computers."

☺

Popular Mechanics forecasting the relentless march of science in 1949: "Computers in the future may weigh no more than 1.5 tons."

An editor in charge of business books for Prentice Hall publishers in 1957: "I have traveled the length and breadth of this country and talked with the best people, and I can assure you that data processing is a fad that won't last out the year."

🔮

An IBM engineer in 1968 asked this plaintive question about the microchip: "But what is it good for?"

Ken Olson, founder of Digital Equipment Corporation, in 1977: "There is no reason anyone would want a computer in their home."

The *New York Daily News* in 1951 about the debut of a new Giant, the future Hall of Famer Willie Mays: "Just so-so in center field."

🔮

Tommy Holmes, minor league baseball manager: "That kid can't play baseball. He can't pull the ball."

Holmes was referring to Hank Aaron, who pulled the ball often enough and far enough to become baseball's all-time home run leader.

Composer Robert Schumann on fellow composer Frederic Chopin: "Nobody can call that music."

Since then we've heard that remark applied to jazz, rock 'n' roll, and rap. It never stops the musicians from making what nobody can call music.

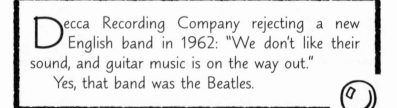

Decca Recording Company rejecting a new English band in 1962: "We don't like their sound, and guitar music is on the way out."

Yes, that band was the Beatles.

Business Week magazine in 1958: "Though import sales could hit 425,000 [cars] in 1959, they may never go that high again."

Within a few years, Japanese carmakers alone would be selling three times that number of cars in the United States.

☺

Steve Jobs on attempts to get major electronics companies to manufacture the personal computer he designed with partner Steve Wozniak: "So we went to Atari and said, 'Hey, we've got this amazing thing, even built with some of your parts, and what do you think about funding us? Or we'll give it to you. We just want to do it. Pay our salary, we'll come work for you.' And they said,

'No.' So then we went to Hewlett-Packard, and they said, 'Hey, we don't need you. You haven't got through college yet.'"

Jobs and Wozniak went on to start Apple Computer.

🔮

A Yale professor explaining the poor grade he gave business student Fred Smith in 1966 for his research paper proposing an overnight delivery system: "The concept is interesting and well-formed, but in order to earn better than a C the idea must be feasible."

After college, Smith founded Federal Express.

🔮

The *Wall Street Journal* a year before Bill Clinton's reelection: "He will lose to any Republican nominee who doesn't drool onstage."

Chapter 4

Popped Culture

Pointing out the stupidities of pop culture seems almost too easy. Still, who can resist?

A movie-theater manager in Seoul, South Korea, found that *The Sound of Music* ran too long. He fixed the problem with some clever editing that hadn't occurred to the musical's director: He cut out the songs.

Paul McCartney woke up one morning humming the melody to what became one of the most popular songs in history, *Yesterday*. Would the song have been as popular if he had kept the original lyrics: "Scrambled eggs. I love your legs"?

There will always be stage mothers, but not many like the woman from Detroit who sent her two daughters (ages eight and ten) on a bus to Hollywood in 1938, telling them to report to central casting, then send for the rest of the family as soon as they became movie stars.

Los Angeles authorities put the girls on the next bus home.

When the TV sitcom *Laverne and Shirley* was syndicated to Thailand, local translators found it necessary to explain the behavior of American sitcom women with the following remark: "The two women depicted in the following episode are from an insane asylum."

Which explains most of what we see on TV.

The producers of the hit TV show Miami Vice spent more money to produce a typical episode than the Miami Police Department spent each year to run the Miami vice squad.

TV's *Sesame Street* became wildly successful by making education enjoyable for young children. But not everyone was happy with that accomplishment.

Professional educators complained that Muppet creator Jim Henson made education too much fun, so that kids found real school boring.

Advice to would-be movie stars: Don't slug the boss if you enjoy the perks of being rich and famous.

Silent-screen star John Gilbert punched out studio chief Louis B. Mayer, one of the most powerful men in Hollywood, over a wisecrack Mayer made when Gilbert was stood up at the altar by actress Greta Garbo.

Mayer swore revenge and got it when talking pictures took over the industry. The mogul convinced Hollywood and the world that Gilbert was through in motion pictures because he had an effeminate voice.

Gilbert drank himself to death within a few years. Mayer went on to become even more extraordinarily rich, powerful, and unsluggable.

Filmmaker Frank Capra's warm-hearted fantasy *It's a Wonderful Life*, one of two all-time favorite holiday movies, bombed at the box office when it was first released in 1946.

The movie was such a failure that years later Capra didn't even bother to renew the copyright. That slipup interested TV stations, which realized they could show the movie without being obligated to pay royalties.

This time around, audiences loved the movie, and *It's a Wonderful Life* became one of the most popular films of all time.

It's hard to break into showbiz, harder still if you try it without the benefit of brains.

In 1929 an aspiring actor named Charles Loeb mailed himself in a box from Chicago to a Hollywood film studio. That gambit got him past the studio gates, but more dead than alive. He recovered from his injuries, but he did not land a part because no one was going to hire anyone that wacko.

Remember that Cinerama epic, *Krakatowa, East of Java*? Only two problems with the title: The volcano is spelled "Krakatoa" and it's not east of Java, it's west. Close enough for Hollywood.

Who was dumber: the studio execs who offered these stars roles they would have been terrible in? Or the stars for turning down roles in movies that became huge hits?

Gary Cooper as Rhett Butler in *Gone with the Wind*.
Robert Redford as Michael Corleone in *The Godfather*.
Anthony Hopkins as Gandhi.
Marlon Brando as Lawrence of Arabia.

Although only 25 percent of Vietnam War veterans have reported problems with battle shock, nearly every single Vietnam vet portrayed in a movie or on a TV show suffers from some form of post-traumatic stress syndrome.

A kids' favorite around the world, the *Muppet Show* was banned in Turkey in 1979 because TV executives there thought Miss Piggy would offend Muslims, who don't eat pork.

In 1956 a TV producer for the U.S. Steel Hour made certain changes in the script for a drama about the true story of a black teenager who was kidnapped and murdered by racists in Mississippi.

The producer, not wanting to cross anyone, changed the black teenager to a Jew, moved the story from the South to New England, and eliminated the murder.

📺

Orson Welles's 1938 radio play, a dramatization of H. G. Wells's *War of the Worlds*, was a ludicrously unbelievable account of a landing and an attack by extraterrestrial aliens.

During the broadcast, the announcers made clear several times that the show was a work of fiction.

Nevertheless, a million listeners thought that space aliens really had invaded the United States. People panicked in the streets.

Two people in Kansas City went to the hospital with alien-inspired heart attacks, while fifteen people in Newark, New Jersey, were treated for shock. One Pittsburgh woman tried to poison herself so the aliens wouldn't get her.

📺

When the crossword puzzle was invented in 1913, it became a worldwide craze, particularly in the United States and England. One of the major side effects of the craze: a tremendous boost in the sale of dictionaries.

Yet dictionaries, being instruments of snobs at the time, refused for seventeen years to recognize that *crossword* was a word.

A Los Angeles radio station informed a woman who called into one of their phone-in shows that the station had a policy that only calls from people under the age of fifty got on the air.

A Florida news anchor interrupted her morning broadcast in 1974 to announce, "In keeping with Channel 40's policy of bringing you the latest in blood and guts, and in living color, you are going to see another first—attempted suicide."

She then pulled out a gun and shot herself on air.

British movie director Tony Kaye brought a monk, a rabbi, and a priest into the New Line studio to help him negotiate to have his name taken off his first film, *American History X.*

"I want to put the fear of God into every production company in this industry," Kaye explained.

Rock singer Carl Perkins's most popular song was *Blue Suede Shoes.* Late in his career, he put on blue suede shoes for all of his concerts.

He wore the showy shoes with dread because after the performance fans would mob the stage to step on his blue suede shoes, exactly as the song urged them not to do.

"You can't believe how much of a problem that becomes," Perkins reported. "My feet get horribly sore. . . . I've seen my fans get older, which means they put on weight, so every year it seems my feet get crushed more."

To promote a bad romantic movie, *The Love Letter*, DreamWorks studio mailed anonymous mash notes to film critics around the country. The letter told the critic that the besotted admirer had been watching and worshipping him or her from afar, and had fallen madly in love with him or her.

The letters were typed by hand and mailed in plain envelopes from the cities in which the critics lived, so that the reporters wouldn't suspect that the letters came from a PR agent in Hollywood. This in an industry whose stars are regularly stalked, and sometimes murdered, by adoring fans.

An Indian movie producer decided to set a record by producing a feature film in twenty-four hours. He hired fifteen directors, fourteen to shoot the film and one to shoot the making of the film. The producer had no script, but gave the actors the idea of what he wanted and then let the cameras roll.

This effort came as no surprise in India, where record setting is such a passion that a man set a record by slicing a cucumber into 120,000 pieces, while another ate a brick in thirty minutes and thirty-three pounds of salt in five days.

How far can *Star Wars* mania go? Anyone can stand in line for three days to see a movie. But a twenty-eight-year-old father of three from Tucson, Arizona, showed real commitment: He legally changed his name to Obi-Wan Kenobi, the Jedi knight played by Alec Guinness in the original movie and Ewan McGregor in the prequel.

In 1949 Harry Cohn, head of Columbia Pictures, dumped a young actress because she had no star quality. Actually, he probably dumped many young actresses. This one turned out to be Marilyn Monroe.

The movies made comic Charlie Chaplin such a huge star that he became one of the founders of United Artists studio and assumed control of his own art. Therefore, we might be surprised that the great clown missed the significance of movies entirely.

"The cinema is little more than a fad," Chaplin explained in 1918. "What audiences really want to see is flesh and blood on the stage."

Here are some other farsighted know-nothings who looked greatness squarely in the face and missed it completely:

1. Rock-band manager Eric Easton helped put together the Rolling Stones in 1963. He told the band there was one thing holding them back. "The singer will have to go," Easton explained, referring to the gawky Mick Jagger.

2. "That the character Snow White is a failure in every way is undisputable," critic V. F. Calverton wrote about the 1938 debut of Walt Disney's first full-length animated film. "Another Snow White will sound the Disney death-knell."

3. "Displays no trace of imagination, good taste or ingenuity," film critic Russell Maloney wrote in the *New Yorker*

in 1939. "I say it's a stinkeroo." Maloney was referring to *The Wizard of Oz*.

4. "Hollywood often uses its best players, writers and directors for its epic phonies," Manny Farber observed in the *New Republic* in 1942. "Warner's is *Casablanca*."

5. "This is third-rate Hitchcock," Dwight Macdonald declared in Esquire in 1960. He meant *Psycho*.

6. "As difficult to sit through as a Black Mass sung in Latin," Michael Sragow complained in the *Los Angeles Herald Examiner* in 1979, referring to one of the most exciting thrillers of all time, *Alien*.

7. "Murphy's aggressive one-upsmanship through most of the film kills your interest in him as a performer," Pauline Kael commented in the *New Yorker* about Eddie Murphy in *Beverly Hills Cop*, the film that made him one of the most popular movie stars in the world.

8. "Spielberg . . . may indeed have made the most monumental molehill in movie history," John Simon predicted in 1982, condemning one of Spielberg's huge hits, *Close Encounters of the Third Kind*.

9. "The biggest disappointment of 1965. . . . The film bumbles along to boredom," Andrew Sarris wrote in the *Village Voice* about *Dr. Zhivago*.

10. "If sharks can yawn, that's presumably what this one is doing," Stanley Kauffmann said about *Jaws* in the *New Republic*. "It's certainly what I was doing all through this picture."

11. "The film is simply a bore. . . . So save your money," Christopher Hitchens advised *New Statesman* readers who might be tempted to see *Raiders of the Lost Ark*.

12. "A standard-issue baby-faced actor," David Denby

declared, dismissing the star of *Risky Business*, Tom Cruise, in *New York* magazine in 1983.

13. "Not only can he not act, he cannot even look and sound halfway intelligent," was how John Simon blasted the star of *The Deep*, Nick Nolte, in 1977

14. "How a society as dynamic as our own throws up such a monstrosity is beyond the scope of this review," Henry Hart wrote about Elvis Presley in the movie *Love Me Tender.*

15. "At no time are we watching a young man who demonstrates a natural or exciting flair for dancing," Gary Arnold commented in the *Washington Post* about John Travolta in the disco movie that made his career, *Saturday Night Fever.*

16. "And then there is Diane Keaton's scandalous performance," John Simon wrote in *New York* magazine in 1977. "It is not so much an actress playing a role as a soul in torment crying out for urgent therapy—in bad taste to watch and an indecency to display."

Simon was referring to Keaton's star turn in *Annie Hall*, the role for which she won an Oscar.

One movie star saw clearly through the fog that seemed to dim the bulbs of so many others. "People don't credit me with much of a brain," Sylvester Stallone said. "So why should I disillusion them?"

Tex Antoine, New York's popular TV weatherman, lost his job after beginning a report with this remark: "It is well to remember the words of Confucius: 'If rape is inevitable, lie back and enjoy it.'"

The dumbest mistake many moviemakers commit is making them in the first place. The following films incorporated some swell oversights, proving that no matter how gigantic your budget and your ego, you can make the smallest error and it will last for years.

1. In *The Wrong Box*, a story set in Victorian England, you can see numerous TV antennas on the rooftops of London.

2. In *Carmen Jones*, as actress Dorothy Dandridge walks down the street, you can track the camera and sound crew walking with her by their reflections in a store window.

3. During the big car chase in *Bullitt*, Steve McQueen's car loses three hubcaps. Later when the chase ends with his car crashing into a wall, three more hubcaps fly off.

4. Alec Guinness won an Oscar for *The Bridge on the River Kwai*, but his name was misspelled as "Guiness" in the credits.

5. In *Goonies*, a kid remarks that his favorite adventure was fighting the octopus. Only they never fought the octopus because the big octopus fight ended up on the cutting-room floor.

6. In *Jailhouse Rock*, Elvis Presley must have been sent to prison for multiple crimes because in one scene he wears a shirt identifying him as prisoner No. 6240. In the next scene, he's prisoner No. 6239.

In 1963 the producers of a movie called *Four for Texas*, a comedy about the Old West starring Frank Sinatra and the Rat Pack, screen-tested actresses in the nude, then shot nude scenes with the actresses who won the roles.

The producers knew the censors would cut out all the nude scenes, which had nothing to do with the rest of the story, before the film was released.

The movie *Heaven's Gate* would have been a flop for one simple reason: It was a lousy movie. But it took some real effort to turn it into a megaflop.

A loser of gigantic proportions requires, most of all, a director losing his grip.

Michael Cimino, who directed the epic Western, demanded millions of dollars' worth of authenticity. He spent megabucks on a wagon train with eighty wagons, hundreds of horses, and 1,200 extras who had to be taught how to ride, drive wagons, and use bullwhips.

He built a gigantic skating rink, and paid for 250 extras to take lessons on the use of antique ice skates. He rented a yacht, a brass band, and an authentic nineteenth-century train, which had to be rerouted from Denver to Idaho because it was too large for twentieth-century train tunnels.

Throw all that—plus twenty retakes of simple scenes and 1.5 million feet of film—into a bad movie and you've got the kind of legendary blunder that makes Hollywood the envy of million-dollar idiots the world over.

Chapter 5

Dumb Ways to Die

As dull as we grow in our daily routines, we show vast ingenuity in finding new and stupid ways to get ourselves killed.

Life's partner in crime, death, has always been a fast worker. But some people go out of their way to find death before death finds them.

A South Korean wife hanged herself in humiliation in 1987. The source of her shame? She had forgotten to set her clock ahead when the country switched to daylight savings time, and her husband had to leave for the company picnic without his lunch.

A drunk security guard asked a fellow worker at a Moscow bank to stab his bulletproof vest to see if it would protect him against a knife attack. It didn't.

An Alabama man died from rattlesnake bites after playing snake catch with a friend.

A sixteen-year-old English boy deodorized himself to death because he was obsessed with smelling nice. The coroner said the boy suffered a heart attack because he had ten times the lethal dose of propane and butane in his blood, built up from spraying his body for months with extreme amounts of deodorant.

🪦

In 1841 England's greatest daredevil, Samuel Scott, performed stunt acrobatics while hanging by a rope with the noose around his neck from London's Waterloo Bridge.

One day the noose slipped. Scott strangled to death on the bridge while the audience cheered, assuming it was part of the act.

🪦

So many rock stars die young, you'd think it was a career move. They kill themselves in car crashes, plane crashes, drug crashes. They overdose on booze and overstuffed sandwiches.

Then there was Terry Kath, lead singer for Chicago, one of the hot bands of the '70s. Playing with a gun, Kath pointed it at his head. His famous last words to friends were, "Don't worry. It's not loaded. See?"

🪦

A seventy-three-year-old man died of exposure during the freezing winter of 1989 in Rochester, New York, when he became stuck in a trash can on his own front porch.

People who passed by thought he was just fooling around, so no one stopped to help.

In 1933 a Japanese schoolgirl killed herself by jumping into an active volcano. Her death started a fad, with more than three hundred other Japanese children killing themselves the same way.

Tourists flocked to the island to watch people jump into the volcano. Police finally stopped the fad by erecting fences around the crater and making it illegal to buy a one-way ticket to the island.

A Florida woman with a genius IQ of 189 was so worried about dying of stomach cancer that she drank four gallons of water a day. She died at the age of twenty-nine of kidney failure.

In 1857 a South African girl of the Gcealeka Xhosa tribe had a vision that if her people destroyed all their worldly possessions, the spirits would lead them to glorious victory over the white men who had stolen their country.

Her tribe followed the girl's vision, destroyed everything they owned, and 25,000 of them starved to death.

A veteran skydiver who was also a cameraman filmed the exploits of fellow skydivers with a camera strapped to his helmet. So it must have come as quite a surprise to the pro when he jumped out of a plane in April 1988, after having remembered to load and adjust his camera but forgetting to put on his parachute.

Actress Peg Entwistle, twenty-four, despairing of ever becoming a movie star, jumped to her death off the H in the famous Hollywood sign in 1932.

After her death, a friend opened a letter that had just arrived in the mail. The letter was from a movie producer, offering Entwistle a role in a picture. She would have played a girl who commits suicide.

🪦

Every golfer alive will relate to the impulse behind this stupid death in 1982 when a New Orleans golfer, playing badly on the 13th hole, threw his club away in disgust. The club hit his golf cart and broke in two. The shaft rebounded off the cart and stabbed the golfer in the neck, severing his jugular vein.

🪦

Army deserter Richard Paris went to Vegas on his honeymoon in 1967. He used fourteen sticks of dynamite to blow himself up, along with his bride and five other honeymooners.

🪦

Famed playwright Tennessee Williams suffocated to death at the age of seventy-one when he bent his head back to squirt in nose spray, the cap fell into his mouth, and he partially swallowed it.

Writers should watch what they swallow. Sherwood Anderson died at sixty-four when peritonitis set in after he swallowed a snack at a party but didn't remove the toothpick first.

Barnstorming pilot Lincoln Beachey decided his aerial stunts were growing too dangerous. Before he went looping, he strapped himself into the plane so he wouldn't fall out and kill himself.

Losing a wing during a dive, his plane crashed into San Francisco Bay. He drowned because he couldn't get free of the straps.

🪦

Henry Flagler, one of the founders of Standard Oil, died in 1913, attacked by his own door. The millionaire built himself a mansion in Florida, complete with fancy automatic doors. One of the closing doors caught him from behind and knocked him down the stairs. He died from the injuries.

🪦

Doesn't it make you mad when your team loses a close game it should have won? It made plenty of Peruvian soccer fans mad in 1964 when Argentina beat the national team on a disputed last-minute goal. Three hundred angry fans were killed in the ensuing riot.

That's small-time fatal stupidity compared to the riot that started 1,400 years ago over an unpopular call in a Constantinople chariot race. That riot claimed 30,000 lives. No record exists of whether the umpire was among them.

🪦

When Sherlock Holmes's creator, Arthur Conan Doyle, turned to lecturing about the spirit world, his speeches were so convincing that several New Yorkers who heard him speak at Carnegie Hall killed themselves so they could get to the spirit world sooner.

In 1929 firemen in Kent, England, put on a public demonstration of their skills, using nine young boys as pretend victims to be rescued from a burning house.

One of the firemen forgot the smoke bombs they had planned to use and actually set fire to the house. All the boys died in the blaze, while the crowd cheered, thinking the boys were actually dummies.

🪦

In Liverpool, England, an elderly man was following his 224-pound wife up the stairs one night in 1903. She lost her balance and fell backward, hit her head on the floor, and died instantly.

Her husband lay trapped under her body for three days. By the time friends found them, he had also died.

In 1983 a San Diego woman, arrested for shoplifting, swore she would hold her breath until she turned blue if the police didn't release her. They didn't, she did, and she died.

To commemorate the death of the Great Houdini, Joe Burrus, a latter-day escape artist, tried to better one of Houdini's stunts in 1990. He was chained and locked, then buried in a clear plastic coffin. Seven tons of concrete were poured on top of the coffin. But before Burrus could escape, the weight of the concrete crushed the coffin and he died on the same day as the master himself.

When silent-screen star Rudolph Valentino died at the age of thirty in 1926, a New York woman shot herself, an English actress poisoned herself, and two Japanese women committed suicide by volcano.

None of the women had ever met Valentino. They had all fallen for him in the movies.

When James Dean died young while speeding in his sports car, he sparked another round of fan suicide.

🪦

Two Parisians fought a duel with muskets in hot-air balloons in 1808. One man shot the other man's balloon, and his rival died from the plunge.

🪦

The *London Times* reported the accidental death of a boy who was rowing in the Mersey River with his friend in 1869. The boat capsized. The boy couldn't swim. Every time his friend tried to rescue him, the boy's dog bit him, trying to protect his master from attack. The master drowned.

🪦

An Australian man was shooting pool in his garage when he thought up a cute trick shot. He hoisted himself onto a ceiling crossbeam and hung by his feet while he cued up.

He fell, hit his head on the concrete, and died of brain damage, although he may have suffered the brain damage prior to the fall.

In 1901 Maud Willard threw herself over Niagara Falls in a barrel, but the fall didn't kill her as it has other daredevils.

What got Maud? She forced her dog into the barrel with her. The dog pressed its nose up against the barrel's single air vent, and Maud suffocated.

RIP

The Austrian Hans Steininger proudly held the sixteenth-century record for the world's longest beard. One day, while climbing up the stairs, he tripped on his beard and died from the fall.

Patients from a Cleveland mental institution were evacuated during a 1933 fire. Nine of the women patients went back inside to get out of the cold. They burned to death.

🪦

It's all fun and games during spring break at Daytona Beach, Florida, unless death plays along.

In 1989 an Illinois college student on spring break was playing the popular motel sport of balcony Frisbee. He leaned out too far for a catch and fell to his death. His is the only recorded fatality to mar the pacific sport of Frisbee.

Jessie Sharp was an expert kayaker, so good he thought he could kayak over Niagara Falls. Which he did in 1990, but only once.

🪦

In Mortar, Italy, a dog shot and killed its master. The man was out hunting when his dog fell into a ditch. When the hunter held out his rifle to help the dog up, it pawed the trigger.

🪦

In Sunderland, England, a twenty-seven-year-old man was rushed to the hospital after reporting difficulty breathing. The man had glued his nostrils shut after confusing a bottle of glue with nasal spray.

🪦

Coworkers in Stafford, England, wanted to do something special for their pal's fiftieth birthday, so they threw him a party, even hired an exotic dancer to pop out of a cake.

The man got the shock of his life when the naked dancer who popped out turned out to be his daughter. The shock proved too much for the birthday boy, who dropped dead from a heart attack.

🪦

Two brothers in Los Angeles decided to remove a bees' nest from a backyard shed by blowing it up with an illegal firecracker. They lit the fuse and ran back inside their house. The explosion blew in a window, cutting up one of the brothers badly enough to require stitches.

When the brothers headed toward their car, the wounded one was stung three times by the surviving bees. Neither of them knew that the stung brother was allergic to bee venom. They found out too late when he died of suffocation on the way to the hospital.

🪦

A Minneapolis man was charged with murder in the death of his cousin. The two young men were playing a game of Russian roulette and used a semiautomatic pistol.

A New Jersey man choked to death on a sequined pastie he had removed with his teeth from an exotic dancer's costume. "I didn't think he was going to eat it," the dancer told police. "He was really drunk."

Two Canadian friends died in a head-on collision, earning a tie in the game of chicken they were playing with their snowmobiles.

🪦

A Frenchman tried a complex suicide in 1998. Standing on a tall cliff, he tied a noose around his neck, securing the rope to a large rock. He then drank poison and set fire to himself. As he jumped off the cliff, he fired a pistol at his head.

The bullet missed him and cut through the rope so he didn't hang himself when he plunged into the sea. And not only did the cold water extinguish his burning clothes, but the shock of it made him vomit up the poison.

He was dragged out of the water by a fisherman and taken to a hospital, where he died of hypothermia.

🪦

A West Virginia fast-food worker died while trying to use short, tie-down straps to bungee jump off a seventy-foot railroad trestle.

The man taped several of the straps together, wrapped one end around his foot, and anchored the other end to the trestle. Then he jumped.

But as police explained, the length of the cord that he had assembled was greater than the distance between the trestle and the pavement below.

🪦

An Austrian circus dwarf was performing trampoline stunts at an outdoor show in Zambia when he took a bad bounce and landed in the yawning mouth of a hippopotamus. Half swallowed, the man suffocated before the hippo's jaws could be pried open.

Chapter 6

Stupid Inventions

For every lightbulb we invent, a dozen guys are working on a dozen versions of self-contained, firefly-powered illumination devices.

Stupid inventions often demonstrate as much ingenuity and hard work as the inventions that change the world. Inventors of useless, ridiculous, and totally idiotic contraptions miss genius rank on a single fault. They could not answer the question: What in the world ever made you think we needed something like that?

Although they never took the world by storm or otherwise, patents were awarded to: a rocking chair–powered vacuum cleaner, a rocking chair–powered butter churn, a yegg-proof safe that exploded when it was opened, an army helmet with a gun on top that soldiers fired by blowing into a pneumatic tube, a cannon that shot live snakes at the enemy, and a submarine aircraft carrier.

Let's not forget these other perfectly brilliant but stupid inventions:

Railroad trains built with rails on top of every car.

The idea was when a fast train caught up to a slower train on the same track, it could pass by climbing up atop the slow train, rolling over the cars, and sliding down the other end.

51

Eyeglasses for chickens, so that other chickens wouldn't peck their eyes out.

Shoulder braces for hats. The braces enabled you to transfer the weight of the hat from your head to your shoulders, thus permitting "free circulation of air entirely around and over the head of the wearer," according to the patent application.

These metal hat supports would subsequently afford an "unobstructed exhibition of the ornamentation and trimming of the wearer's hair."

As would not wearing a hat.

In 1884 a Brit named Harry Fell was granted a government patent for making gold from wheat. His plan: Soak the wheat in water for ten hours, then dry the liquid, which turns into gold.

Fell may not have been a fool, only ahead of his time. Farmers subsequently perfected the technique of turning nonwheat into gold by getting the government to pay them not to farm.

A mechanical buggy whip that enabled a wagon driver to apply the whip to any horse in the team in only seven easy steps, none of which involved the manual snapping of the whip.

Breath-powered foot warmers. This apparatus was fashioned from tubes that ran inside your shirt, then bifurcated down each pant leg.

The top of the tube plugged into a funnel that strapped under your chin, into which you exhaled. The warmth of your exhalations floated down the tubes, keeping your feet toasty on cold days and strangers at a safe distance.

A dimple maker that worked on the principle of the rotary hand drill.

A mechanical baby patter to help put tots to sleep by patting them on the butt.

The patter was to be used in conjunction with the automatic baby-burping apparatus, which looked like one of those circus props used for launching acrobats.

A two-person topcoat for snuggling on cold days.

A movie theater in which the audience entered and exited through trap doors under each seat so they wouldn't step on one another's toes going out to the candy counter.

A cow decoy for hunters, which enabled two men to hide inside and wait for their unsuspecting prey—or a bull.

An automatic hair-cutting machine, whose use was to be followed by the automatic scalp-massaging machine, which required the user to stand on his head inside the apparatus.

A farm plow with a rifle welded onto the blade so that a man could farm and fire at the same time when the need arose.

A giant hot-air balloon powered by eagles. Or if you preferred, by vultures or condors.

A fishing lure in the shape and design of a naked woman, presumably used to lure sharks.

A rotary, gear-operated, automatic hat tipper designed to enable men to keep their hands free while tipping their hats politely with a nod of the head.

A combination cheese grater and mousetrap.

A smelly navigation system to help ships sail in fog without crashing into one another.

Each ship would be equipped with pumps that would propel nauseating odors to warn other ships of its presence.

Thick elastic shoes for jumping out of burning buildings. When you landed on your feet in the street below, the elastic would absorb the impact.

If you had to jump out of a particularly tall building, you simply added the accompanying parachute to your personal safety system. The chute fit neatly on top of your head and was held in place by a strap under your chin.

A jet-powered surfboard, intended, no doubt, for use in slow oceans.

Fake sideburns attached to sunglasses for the Elvis look.

A car burglar alarm that combined a detection circuit with a flamethrower.

A self-perfuming business suit.

A rifle that pitched baseballs, invented by a professor in 1897. It was intended to replace unreliable pitchers who couldn't get the ball over the plate often enough.

Strangely enough, the pitching rifle was actually tried in games. Even stranger, it wasn't pitchers who convinced the commissioner to ban the rifle from baseball. Batters didn't like it because without the motion of the pitcher's arm they couldn't pick up the pitch.

🙊

In 1953 a skier tired of waiting in long lift lines, invented self-propelled skis that powered skiers uphill. The device required skiers to fit belts under their skies and strap gas engines to their backs.

The power ski never took off because no one could figure out what the skier would do with the backpack engine at the top of the hill.

🙊

Dozens of inventors have created dozens of ways to help golfers find lost golf balls. The continued prevalence of lost golf balls will testify to the success of these attempts:

1. Coating golf balls with chemicals that would cause insects to swarm to the ball, thus identifying its location for the insect repellent–coated golfer.
2. Injecting odiferous chemicals into golf balls so golfers could sniff out their lost drives.
3. Inserting a tiny amount of radioactive chemicals inside the ball so it would click when the golfer approached with a Geiger counter.

If this device had ever been used, it would have replaced lost golf balls with lost golfers.

The Hun warriors of the fourth century invented the fearsome visage as a psychological weapon of war.

To strike fear into their enemies, the Huns would bind the heads of their infant boys so that by the time they grew old enough to fight they had deformed faces.

A tricycle with a printing press attached to the rear wheels that printed two different advertisements on the street as you rode along.

This device was designed in 1895 before the advent of the traffic jam.

A mechanical swimming bicycle upon which the pedaling swimmer lay supine, cranking with both hands and feet to turn a propeller that moved you through the water.

A flying machine in which the pilot rode inside a cage attached to a circular frame. The machine was carried through the air by a dozen eagles strapped into leather jackets hooked onto the frame.

A complete lifesaving system consisting of a flotational body suit that kept a shipwrecked swimmer vertical in the water for days.

The suit was outfitted with drinking water, food, torches, rockets, cigars, and reading material to help pass the time until rescuers arrived.

In 1891 a French engineer designed a daredevil ride specifically for the Eiffel Tower.

The ride consisted of a gigantic, bullet-shaped chamber big enough to seat fifteen people. The chamber would be hoisted to the top of the Eiffel Tower, then dropped to free fall into a champagne glass–shaped reservoir of water at the bottom of the tower.

The effect of the adventure, although it was never built, was described as a thrill. Something may have been lost in the translation from the French.

A machine for electroplating corpses was invented in 1891, so that you could coat your loved ones in a millimeter of copper and put them on display in their favorite easy chairs.

In 1886 two German brothers invented the photographic hat, consisting of a camera bolted inside a hat, to make cameras more portable.

A folding stool sewn inside the bustle of a nineteenth-century lady's skirts, which automatically unfolded into a seat when the lady sat down and folded back up for easy storage when she stood up.

A diet feedback tape that played antieating messages every time you opened your fridge.

A long-distance, pest-killing machine called the Coetherator. A farmer would take a picture of his field, put the photo in the machine, and fill it with insecticide. The machine would then kill the pests miles away from the field.

Bad food concoctions (most of them promoted by food marketing groups trying to increase sales of their product) aren't the same thing as bad food, although they can be.

But how would you know that any of the following foods were bad? You weren't actually going to try grape pesto pizza, peanut butter and Jell-O sandwiches, berries with green peppercorn sauce, pear-and-tomato pizza, tongue salad with cherries and hard-boiled eggs, spaghetti-squash waldorf salad, peanut-stuffed prune salad, onion wine, jalapeño pepper ice cream, cheeseburger-flavored popcorn, or fig ice cream?

Even geniuses aren't always so bright. When Thomas Edison invented the first phonograph in 1877, he wasn't thinking about the gigantic music industry he had just created. He thought the phonograph would be used as a device for people to record messages that would then be sent from one central telephone office to another, much the way people sent telegrams.

It took the public sixteen years to convince Edison that the phonograph had a future in the music business.

Many of the inventions mentioned above actually won patents. Historically, an idea didn't have to be doable to be patented. It only had to be unique, which was often its best feature.

These ideas and many others so impressed the man in charge of the U.S. Patent Office that he resigned, suggesting that the office be closed since there was nothing left to invent.

The year: 1875.

Chapter 7

Stupid Social Customs

When we look back far enough, we find the beliefs held by people in earlier societies to be stupid, foolish, and blatantly false. Yet we confidently hold our own beliefs to be obviously true.

At least we won't be around in a few hundred years to hear them laughing at us. So let's laugh backward:

In Victorian England proper library etiquette demanded that books written by women not be shelved next to books written by men, unless the authors were married to each other.

In the twelfth century, Europeans believed that trees gave birth to birds.

For centuries, until Magellan's ships circumnavigated the globe, Europeans believed that no people could possibly live on the other side of the earth, even if it *was* round.

Forget about people falling off the bottom of the planet, this belief was religious, and was proved theologically.

If there were people on the other side of the earth, the intelligentsia reasoned, they wouldn't be able to see Jesus arrive at the Second Coming. Since God wanted everyone to witness that event at the same time, He wouldn't allow people to live out of sight of it.

For thousands of years comets were presumed to be condensations of people's sins. That's why they brought pestilence, famine, war, and the death of kings.

In medieval France priests and judges maintained that animals could be possessed by Satan. On the gallows in the French countryside, cows and pigs were hung by the neck until dead to release the devil within.

Because the meat of convicted stock was sinful, cow corpses were burned, not butchered. Thus, people starved while watching their farm animals slaughtered but not used for food.

We're much too civilized to condone such stupidity today. But in 1916, a circus elephant that killed three men was lynched using a railroad derrick and steel cables to hang her.

When high heels were invented in France in 1590, they were worn by men, who used them to assume a position of power over other men.

Men soon found that dominance was difficult to maintain when you were falling down after every other step.

So high heels were passed on to women, where they became a symbol of sexual subservience. Upper-class women wore heels to demonstrate that they were too rich to have to move.

During the French Revolution, women abandoned their heels as elitist. In a counterrevolutionary gesture, ballerinas started dancing on their toes to simulate high heels.

In the seventeenth and eighteenth centuries, rich men showed their class stature by shaving all the hair off their heads, then donning elaborate powdered wigs.

The wigs were often made from the hair of dead poor people, which was the cheapest way for wig makers to gather supplies.

Human sacrifice was once practiced by religions all over the world, as a ritual that brought their people a little closer to God, with the person being sacrificed a little closer than everyone else.

The early Babylonians sacrificed animals on their altars. Then priests would read God's will in the dead animal's liver. Why? The Babylonians thought the liver was the home of the soul.

The ancient goddess Cybele of Anatoli was popular with devout Romans in the second century B.C. The Romans worshipped her by bathing in the blood of sacrificed bulls.

The Catholics did it. So did the Protestants. They lashed heretics and witches by the thousands to stakes, set them aflame, and watched them burn. Isn't that a human sacrifice? It was to the poor people who were burned.

What exactly is a witch or a heretic? Anyone you burn at the stake in the name of God.

In the 1700s English judges would test accused witches by drowning them. If a woman was a real witch, the water would reject her, they reasoned. Therefore, all a woman had to do to prove her innocence was drown.

Thousands of innocent women died that way.

The branding of women as witches possessed by the devil continued over several hundred years in England, France, Germany, Spain, Italy, and the American colonies. Under the direction of men of God, these women were tortured until they confessed, at which point they were killed.

Anyone who tried to suggest that these women weren't witches and that the Church should stop torturing and killing women in the name of the Prince of Peace was tortured and killed in the name of the Prince of Peace.

In the eighteenth century the London hospital for the insane, called Bedlam, raised money by charging Londoners admission to see cages filled with chained prisoners, a human zoo.

The ancient Aztecs of Mexico honored people in religious ceremonies by sending them to the gods, which meant they first had to get rid of their bodies, as that was the only way to get there.

To prepare people for the sacred journey, Aztec priests would cut open the lucky travelers' chests and rip out their hearts. To dedicate a new temple, the Aztec king Ahuitzotl sacrificed 80,000 hearts to the gods.

Throughout the Middle Ages it was believed that certain kings had the power to heal the sick by touch. In 1684 a mass of the lame and the ill gathered to be touched by King Charles II of England.

The crowd grew so large and eager for kingly salvation that seven people were cured of their diseases by being trampled to death.

In Alexandria in the second century there was a law against women tricking men into marriage by applying makeup to deceive the men about their looks.

In our age men trick women into marriage by asking them.

If September is the ninth month of the year, why do we call it the seventh? We also get October, November, and December wrong.

The names of these months in Latin mean seven, eight, nine, and ten, respectively, but they are our ninth, tenth, eleventh, and twelfth months.

Well, we came close.

It worked out that way because March used to be the first month of the year. By that system, September was the seventh, October the eighth, and the other two followed in order.

But when the first month of the year was changed to January, the names of the last four months were not changed. Why? Because that's the way we are.

🃏

The Cracker Jack people have packed more than 16 billion toys in their boxes of candied popcorn since 1912. Aside from collectors, almost nobody still has any of them.

In seventeenth-century Europe, sneezing was considered a sign of good breeding. That's why members of the upper classes started sniffing snuff: to promote sneezing so they could demonstrate their superiority.

In France in the 1600s the remains of executed murderers were considered good-luck charms. Crowds would gather to pick apart the charred remains of people beheaded and burned, ignoring the obvious fact that these murderers had not been lucky for their victims or, ultimately, for themselves.

Today's hair extremes have nothing on eighteenth-century England, where fashionable women sported wigs up to four feet high. Hairdressers decorated these wigs with stuffed birds, fruit plates, and model ships.

To support such a structure of hair, the women had to sleep sitting up. To hold such elaborate hair sculptures together, the wigs were matted with lard. Since women often wore the wigs continuously for months, the lard attracted insects and mice.

A fad among Englishwomen in the late nineteenth century: nipple rings. The women believed the rings would enhance the size and shape of their breasts.

For most of recorded history, Europeans wrote without vowels. Reading was guesswork.

For example, the English word written *grnd* could mean grand, grind, or ground.

Vowel guesswork was haphazard and a silly method of writing for people trying to communicate. But the Europeans compounded their thickness by writing their sentences crammed together without spaces between the words.

In the Middle Ages Chinese peasants built homes in caves they dug out of soft clay. When a powerful earthquake hit northern China in 1556, the walls of a cave city were so weakened that 800,000 people were buried alive inside their cave homes.

The plague of the fourteenth century led to a confounding attempt at disease prevention in Germany and France: Flagellants marched from town to town, lashing one another with metal-tipped whips.

Their theory was that public atonement for sins would spare them from the Black Death. This method of plague control worked particularly well for the flagellants who died from excessive blood loss due to overenthusiastic whipping.

The Spanish Inquisition treated people like animals and vice versa. Believing that witches inhabited the bodies of cats, the Church ordered thousands of cats destroyed.

A popular pastime in sixteenth-century Paris was the public burning of bagfuls of cats to celebrate Midsummer Day.

In the seventeenth century pointed table knives were declared illegal in France. Why? Cardinal Richelieu was offended by the sight of uncouth diners picking their teeth with their knife points.

That's why, in our time, we use knives with rounded ends at table.

In the Middle Ages Spanish nobles found Spanish ladies difficult to kiss because the women always kept sharp toothpicks in their mouths all day and night.

In medieval times, when people ate out of a common dish, it was considered uncouth to gnaw on a bone and then throw it back in the pot for others to pick at. It was also considered low class to spit across the table or blow your nose on the tablecloth.

While knives and spoons were popular throughout the Western world, forks were generally unknown until the eleventh century. Instead, people took food from the common dish with their hands.

You could tell a nobleman from a peasant because the upper class washed their hands first and didn't take meat that displeased them from their mouths and put it back in the pot.

When a Byzantine noblewoman tried to introduce the use of the fork into Venetian society, she created a scandal. She was deemed overly refined. When she became ill, religious leaders declared that she was being punished by God for her sin of the fork.

In sixteenth-century Italy a proper gentleman did not wash his hands after relieving himself because the washing would remind decent people of the business he had just been about.

At the height of their civilization, Romans considered stuffed mice a dinner delicacy.

In some African cultures a woman's sex appeal was determined by the size and shape of the gap between her upper two front teeth. Some women, unlucky enough to be born gapless, would file down their teeth to achieve that gappy look.

No telling how long before Beverly Hills plastic surgeons pick up on that status symbol.

In Colonial America people thought they could cure stomachaches by placing big boots on their bellies.

Among the people of northern Spain, a village's babies were placed on the ground and a man, symbolizing the dangers infants face in life, leaped over them.

If he landed on the other side without landing on the babies, that symbolized their safe passage through the early years. If he didn't, it didn't.

Among the Berber tribes of North Africa, parents arranged marriages for daughters as young as ten. After a five-day wedding ceremony, the young couple was divorced so the daughter could marry someone else.

Among ancient Persians only the king had the right to use an umbrella to ward off sun or rain.

Two thousand years later, the royalty of Siam maintained

their rankings through umbrella status: The higher you stood among the elite, the larger your umbrella and the wider the decorative rings.

In thirteenth-century Germany knights would enter riddle contests that were as serious as jousts. Just as a loser in a tilt often lost his life although it was but a sporting contest, so a knight who could not answer a riddle was often put to death.

This practice may be seen as a primitive way of culling the weak-minded from the stock. But that hardly seemed necessary, as there were already a multitude of opportunities to be killed in the Dark Ages.

Norse followers of the god Odin would hang themselves so they could share the power of their god. One Norse saga recounts the efforts of a woman who hung her son so that Odin would help her brew better ale.

Superstitions about the sacrificial power of death by hanging remained into the nineteenth century, when executioners would sell remnants from hangings as good-luck charms.

English burglars believed that the severed hand of a hung man would enable them to open locks, while a bit of skin from a hanging victim would prevent a house from catching fire.

Among some African tribes, kissing was viewed as a threat of cannibalism because smooching reminded people of the way snakes would tongue victims before dining upon them.

Sailors of the Middle Ages believed that wearing rings in their ears would save them from drowning if their ship sunk.

In ancient Ireland before a king was crowned, he took a bath in the broth prepared from a boiled horse. Ever hear the Irish expression "A broth of a boy"?

When tobacco was introduced to Europe in the sixteenth century, all gentlemen (and some ladies) smoked the plant in pipes. Cigarettes were considered low class, only smoked by beggars who couldn't afford pipes.

Among the ancient Maori, it was believed that scratching the head could release the soul from the body. When you scratched your head, you immediately had to sniff your spirit back into your skull by putting your fingers up your nose.

Chapter 8

Seemed Like a Good Idea at the Time

Let's start an empire. Say, this conquering stuff is fun; pass the wine. Oops, here come the barbarians.

Whether we're emperors or fools, play out a good idea long enough and you might run into that pitfall where smart moves go to stumble.

An antidrug group in New York distributed free pencils to school kids with the antidrug message, "Too Cool to Do Drugs."

It started out okay, but got worse and worse when the kids actually used the pencils. As the pencils were worn down and sharpened, the message changed to: "Cool to Do Drugs." Then: "Do Drugs."

When movie star Warren Beatty directed *Reds* in 1981, he wanted the extras on the set to understand the historical significance of the true story of an American writer who campaigned for workers' rights.

After the director explained the history of the workers' movement, the extras understood his lecture so well that they went on strike against Beatty for higher pay.

🔦

In 1985, to celebrate a year in which no one had drowned in city pools, two hundred New Orleans lifeguards threw a big party. During the party, one of the guests drowned.

🔦

Looking for relief, an Englishman picked up a tube of hemorrhoid cream. Oops, wrong tube. He got the superglue instead, and glued his buns together.

🔦

Inventor Charles Goodyear lived in poverty when he wasn't stuck in debtors' prison because none of his inventions worked. He was a man sparked by ideas that had great promise and no realization.

Failure, debt, doubt, the urge to tinker, and the need to stop tinkering and get an honest job—those were his constant, clashing companions.

Finally, Goodyear promised his wife that he'd stop conducting experiments in their kitchen and find a job that paid the bills.

Of course, he didn't. The man was an inventor. But he knew he was in trouble one day when he heard his wife coming up the stairs, home early. Instead of looking for a job, he'd been experimenting again with attempts to vulcanize rubber.

To avoid antagonizing his wife, he quickly swept his experiment into the kitchen stove. The stove was still hot, which is why Goodyear finally succeeded with one of his crazy experiments, discovering the process for creating heat-resistant rubber.

There's your dumb move turning into a good idea. But despite the importance of that invention, Goodyear died broke anyway.

Oddly, or perhaps not, Goodyear wasn't the only scientist who owed a discovery to a fearsome wife.

German inventor Christian Schönbein discovered smokeless gunpowder when he spilled one of his experiments in his wife's kitchen. Afraid that she would soon return and discover the accident, he mopped up the chemical spill with his wife's apron, then set the apron in front of the fire to dry.

The apron exploded because of cellulose nitration, and Schonbein had a new invention to market.

♥

The founder of the Wrigley chewing-gum empire wasn't a chewing-gum man. William Wrigley, Jr., was trying to make a living in the baking-powder business. To increase sales, he gave away chewing gum to anyone who bought enough of his baking powder. Consumers didn't care for his baking powder, but they liked the gum.

Wrigley recognized a good idea when he stumbled across one and got out of the baking-powder business, with all its frustrations, and into the chewing-gum business.

Later the family spent a good part of its fortune to get into the baseball business by buying the Chicago Cubs, which was when the Wrigleys learned what frustration was really all about.

One man's lame move can make another man's career.

Actor Ronald Reagan got his start in Hollywood when he was hired to replace actor Ross Alexander, who killed himself at the age of twenty-nine.

Reagan later turned down the chance to play Rick in *Casablanca*. If Reagan had been smart enough to take the role, *Casablanca* would have become a forgotten film. And Bogie would have become president.

🔆

Sometimes being dumb pays off. A woman in San Francisco in the 1970s attempted suicide but failed. Put in a hospital room for observation, the woman climbed out of bed, opened the window, and jumped out.

She survived that suicide attempt too. Then she sued the hospital and won damages because they had not put her safely in a room out of which she couldn't have jumped.

A Little Rock, Arkansas, woman wanted to get her driver's license, like everyone else she knew. Unlike everyone else, she failed the written test 103 times—even though you're allowed to study the booklet in the test room right up until you take the test. She finally passed the test on try 104.

Peter the Hermit, a French holy man, led a peasants' crusade at the turn of the eleventh century to seek salvation in Jerusalem. Peter may have been mad, but he gathered a huge following because salvation seemed preferable to the miserable, brutally abrupt life of being a French peasant in the Dark Ages.

The peasants, who took to ravaging villages along their journey to the sea, never made it to the Holy Land, where they would probably have been slaughtered by Saracens. Instead, they were slaughtered by the armies of France, who didn't like the idea of peasants marching, to their salvation or anywhere else.

♥

When the minuet was introduced into French society in the 1600s, it was intended to demonstrate the grace of the upper class.

French dancing masters refined the minuet, which had begun as a folk dance, to the degree that books were written about proper performance. One book contained a lengthy chapter devoted to the correct manner in which the wrist was to be turned and sixty pages explored the details of the gentleman's bow.

♥

Like Buddhist monks around the world, the Chogye order in South Korea practice meditation and nonviolence—except when they deal with one another.

Rival factions of peace-loving monks have been battling for control of the group for years, often erupting into fistfights. In 1999 the Buddhist battle escalated, as monks meditatively beat one another with metal pipes, stones, and bottles.

Ethereal dancer Isadora Duncan made Irish playwright George Bernard Shaw a proposition that sounded good on the face of it: that they have a baby together. "With my body and your brains," she said, "what a wonder it would be."

Shaw turned Isadora down, explaining, "But what if it had my body and your brains?"

🔆

The ABC television network has made millions in advertising by broadcasting *Monday Night Football* over the decades. But the CBS network had first chance to run what has become one of the most popular sports shows of all time.

CBS turned the proposal down, the network president saying, "Preempt Doris Day? Are you out of your mind?"

🔆

Russian scientist Elie Metchnikoff tried to kill himself with an overdose of morphine in 1873 but survived. Seven years later he tried to kill himself again with an injection of deadly bacteria. That didn't work either.

His subsequent research into bacteriology won Metchnikoff a Nobel Prize in 1908.

🔆

William Sidis mastered Latin and Greek by the age of five. At the age of nine, he developed a new method of computing algorithms. He entered Harvard at eleven, graduating at sixteen.

Sidis then spent the rest of his life working as a dishwasher and clerk, amassing one of the world's largest collections of streetcar transfers.

Chapter 9

Government by the Idiots

We get the government we deserve, which doesn't say much for us or them.

In 1975 the head of the Federal Energy Administration flew around the country speaking to business and civic groups about the need to conserve energy.

He spent $25,000 of the taxpayers' money on 19,000 gallons of fuel to spread the word not to waste so much money by using so much fuel.

The federally funded Law Enforcement Assistance Administration spent $27,000 to study why prison inmates want to escape prison.

The U.S. Consumer Products Commission bought 80,000 buttons for a campaign promoting safe toys. The buttons had to be destroyed because they were too sharp and were coated with lead paint.

When President Reagan's daughter Patti got married, there were more police officers and Secret Service agents at the ceremony (180) than there were guests (134).

⚒

In 1658 Virginia passed a law forcing all lawyers to leave the colony, thereby making Virginia as close to Eden as any American territory has come. The law was repealed in 1680. It's been downhill ever since.

⚒

Papal politics reached a new low in 897 when Pope Stephen VI brought Pope Formosus to ecumenical trial, not at all deterred by the fact that Formosus was already dead.

Pope Stephen had his predecessor's corpse seated in the courtroom in purple robes. Pope Formosus was tried and convicted.

⚒

Prior to the French Revolution, a man served fifty years in prison for whistling at Queen Marie Antoinette. Perhaps she shouldn't have been so surprised when she found the peasants revolting.

⚒

After the Clinton-Lewinsky scandal, officials of Madame Tussaud's wax museum in Sydney, Australia, had to seal shut the zipper on the pants of the Clinton dummy. Visitors kept opening it up as a gag.

In 1975 Congress retrofitted the elevators in the Capitol building to make them automatic. Then Congress continued to spend the taxpayers' money to pay the salaries of elevator operators to operate automatic elevators.

The federal government spent nearly $300,000 to build a community center in the woods between two Michigan towns. Money ran out before the roads to the facility could be finished, so no one from either town was able to use their center. It eventually collapsed of disrepair.

It doesn't take a huge federal bureaucracy to accomplish something really dumb. Even the local school board can manage the deed.

A thirteen-year-old Arizona boy was inspired to build a model rocket after seeing the movie *October Sky*, the true story of NASA rocket scientist Homer Hickam. The boy took his rocket, made out of a potato-chip canister and fueled with three match heads, to school.

School officials classified the rocket as a weapon and suspended the boy for the rest of the year, based on its zero-tolerance weapons policy.

Civilian employees at the Seattle Police Department received special training in proper sitting methodology, after two people in the department's fingerprint and photo unit slid off their chairs and fell to the floor.

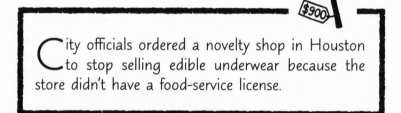

A department supervisor circulated a memo on proper procedures titled "Chairs, How to Sit In." He advised, "Take hold of the arms and get control of the chair before sitting down."

"Some people know how to sit in a chair," a department safety officer explained, while others "need some instruction."

The post office printed a batch of international stamps in 1999 featuring a picture of the Grand Canyon and this message across each stamp: "Grand Canyon, Colorado."

The Grand Canyon is located in Arizona.

City officials ordered a novelty shop in Houston to stop selling edible underwear because the store didn't have a food-service license.

Long considered a pest by western ranchers, prairie dogs are prestigious pets in Japan, where the rodents sell for $30 apiece.

American ranchers would be happy to get rid of the critters, for profit or gratis. But the Colorado Division of Wildlife won't let ranchers export prairie dogs as pets because no species of wildlife may be sold, since they belong to the public. However, because they are considered pests, it's perfectly legal in Colorado to shoot, poison, or drown the prairie dogs.

How well are our government-run schools doing in educating the American people?

The Colonial Williamsburg Foundation put the system to the test with a survey of our historical knowledge.

The survey found that 79 percent of Americans knew that the slogan "Just do it" came from a Nike ad, but only 47 percent knew where "Life, liberty and the pursuit of happiness" came from.

Worse, 55 percent identified Obi-Wan Kenobi as the person who said, "May the force be with you" in *Star Wars*. Only 9 percent knew that George Washington was a general in the Revolutionary War.

The United States government spends billions on defense each year to kill all our enemies, anyone who was thinking of becoming our enemy, and most of the people who just look at us funny.

But the feds also spend countless millions on non-defense: developing new weapons that are never actually put into use. These projects get canceled before completion, but not before costing us millions in tax dollars.

Here are millions of dollars worth of nothing: the B-1A and XB-70 bombers, the ANP nuclear airplane, and the Roland SA, Navaho, Snark, Rascal AS, and Skybolt missiles.

Probably those millions went into deciding upon names for the nonweapons.

The Anglo-Saxons of England initiated an official justice system in the fourth century A.D. Prior to that time, justice was administered by the victor to the victim, following the system known as the Whim. Early Anglo-Saxon justice wasn't much of an improvement.

Under the English system, a man accused of a crime would be forced to close his hand around a poker that had been turned red in a fire. This wasn't the punishment; it was the trial. The man was declared innocent if his wounds healed after three days.

When Caligula was just another struggling assassin trying to move up the Roman ladder of success, a soothsayer told him he'd never make it all the way to emperor, that he had as much chance of getting the top job as he did of riding across the waters of the Bay of Baiae without a boat.

But Caligula was a hard-working assassin. After eliminating the competition, he became emperor of all of Rome, although it was not a position with much job security, even for someone of Caligula's talents.

Upon taking control, Caligula ordered scores of ships lashed together across the three miles of the bay, then covered the ships with wooden planks, piled dirt on top, and rode his horse across the Bay of Baiae.

Three years later he was assassinated by his guards, their way of protesting all the unpaid overtime they put in killing Caligula's enemies.

When the revolutionary tribunals couldn't convict counterrevolutionaries quickly enough following the French Revolution in 1793, the courts simply eliminated such time-consuming legal maneuvers as the defense.

Some 25,000 people were executed for crimes against the state, at which point the people who masterminded the executions were executed.

In 1981 a nine-year-old girl was executed in Iran for attacking government officials. By law, Iranian boys could not be put to death until they turned fifteen.

In an effort to cure the working class of their addiction to gin, the British government passed a law in 1832 officially favoring beer over gin. Workingmen throughout Britain responded to the legislation by drinking beer as a chaser to their gin.

In 1962 a Massachusetts man refused to pay the increased tax on his house. He burned it down instead. The government charged him for the tax increase anyway.

In 1971 a state representative in Rhode Island introduced legislation to charge couples a $2 tax each time they made love. Quickly calculating their own tax liabilities, politicians on both sides of the aisle voted the bill down.

In Yemen in 1968 a pet monkey was tried for arson, convicted, and executed by a police firing squad.

At the same time that the federal government was spending millions of dollars on programs to convince teenagers and others not to kill themselves by smoking cigarettes, Congress authorized a $328 million subsidy to support the nation's tobacco farmers, who were losing money because of the decline in cigarette sales.

The Department of Agriculture found a governmentally clever way to save money on its school lunch programs in the 1980s. The bureaucrats simply declared that they didn't have to buy actual vegetables for nutritionally needy kids because ketchup and relish were vegetables.

In the 1840s the French government passed a law saying that criminals could not be arrested between the hours of sunset and sunrise.

When Harold Ross, publisher of the *New Yorker*, had his fictional magazine character Eustace Tilley registered in the New York City phone book, city administrators sent Tilley a tax bill.

Chapter 10

The Power of Stupidity

King Otto, a nineteenth-century ruler of Bavaria, set the benchmark for the royal class by making it his kingly routine to start each day by shooting a peasant.

Otto and other power-mad rulers may have a tough time convincing anyone of their qualifications for heavenly admittance. But does that mean the persecuted poor can waltz right through the gates as a belated reward for their noble poverty?

The history of power says that given a chance, the amateur despot class turns as cruel and heartless as the usual sadistic suspects.

More dogs have been kicked by the poor than by the rich. Give a poor man a taste of power, and he begins to act as cruelly stupid as the rich man.

For two hundred years in Russia a sect called the Brothers and Sisters of Red Death had a rule against marriage but not against sexual intercourse, as long as the act was followed by suffocating the participants with red pillows.

The sect finally disbanded in 1900 when one hundred members burned themselves to death in anticipation of the millennial end of the world.

In 1358, long before anyone conceived of a popular revolution against a corrupt aristocracy, French peasants suddenly had their fill of being used as pike fodder by the lords of the land.

Tired of being starved, beaten, raped, and killed, the poor actually got off their skinny butts and did something about it. They revolted.

Did they overthrow the aristocracy and start a noble society where everyone was treated as equals, with Christian kindness and respect for the rights of all?

Not in the fourteenth century, they didn't, although they had some trouble getting it right in the fifteenth, sixteenth, seventeenth, eighteenth, nineteenth, and twentieth centuries too.

Meanwhile, back in 1358 the French rebels abused and slaughtered the powerful in a fashion that would have made a king proud. They tied up aristocrats and forced them to watch as their wives and daughters were raped, tortured, and killed.

Within a month, turn-around day was over. The aristocrats brought in better-armed soldiers, and the revolting peasants were put in their place again, at the end of a pike or in the center of a noose.

But the powerless had proven their point: Given the chance, you couldn't tell them apart from the powerful.

⚜

The thirteenth century saw mankind make progress on at least one front: political repression. The most noted scientist of his age, Roger Bacon conceived of telescopes, microscopes, cars, steamships, airplanes, and underwater diving suits, even though there was no technology to support his theories in the 1200s and no labs in which to test them by experiment.

For Bacon's efforts to point the way out of the Dark Ages, the powers that ruled (the council of lords and the Church of the Lord) condemned him to prison.

Prison can wear down even a great visionary so that he sees the futility of his work in a world whose ignorance is insurmountable for the simple reason that the ignorant refuse to be surmounted.

"Would that I had not given myself so much trouble for the love of science," Bacon concluded miserably.

How many other people of illuminating intelligence have reached the same conclusion: that their ability to see what others will not is more of a curse than a blessing?

Is history replete with the silences of people who could have made a difference but chose not to under the pain of persecution?

♔

In the 1850s a Chinese visionary named Hung Hsiu-Ch'uan heard God say that he was the younger brother of Jesus.

To fulfill his vision, Hung organized the God Worship Society, which called for the Christ-like virtues of equality and morality.

Such beliefs can elevate people to moments of religious beneficence, or drive them to acts of vast stupidity. Equality and morality led Hung to declare a war against China's rulers that lasted fourteen years and cost 20 million lives—all in the name of the younger brother of the Prince of Peace.

When his rebellion finally failed, Hung committed suicide. So did 100,000 of his followers, making other religion-based suicides pale in comparison.

What do the following rulers have in common?

1. British prime minister David Lloyd George, who called Adolf Hitler a "great man."
2. Idi Amin, dictator of Uganda, who tried to exterminate the East Indians and Pakistanis in his country, whom he labeled "the Jews of Africa."
3. Nguyen Cao Ky, U.S.-supported premier of South Vietnam, who in the late '60s suggested that he could beat the Viet Cong if his country only had "four or five Hitlers."

No, not just their admiration for the world's most successful lunatic. But the obvious fact, which only rulers a little low on ammunition could miss, that Hitler would have happily exterminated all of them if he had succeeded with his master plan to conquer the world.

♔

Don't get us started on the stupid atrocities of the French and Russian Revolutions, which were supposed to be the second and third wave of glorious rectification of the wrongs of the elite through the enlightened intelligence of the common man.

Those two bloody revolutions do make you wonder why the American Revolution was so relatively free of barbarism.

Actually, even the American Revolution had its share of stupid atrocities. But certainly nothing like the bloodbaths into which the revolutionaries managed to pour themselves in France and Russia.

In the American Revolution, neither side represented the poor. The colonists, led by Franklin, Jefferson, and Washington, were hardly peasants. America was a rich land waiting to be grabbed and they were grabbing.

Because many of the revolutionaries had been born in the new land, they didn't have centuries of hatred to avenge. Angry, would-be mobs lacked a convenient palace to torch. The British aristocracy that the American colonists revolted against were too far away to be dragged through the streets by their throats.

For their part, the British officers knew they were leading an army against people they weren't very much different from.

Still, there was the occasional dumb atrocity, such as the Wyoming Valley massacre in 1778, in which Tories encouraged their Indian allies to torture and slaughter Pennsylvania colonists who had been their neighbors for no particular military objective.

It's only by comparison to other revolutions that the American adventure looks clean.

⚜

The worst acts of revolution belong to those suave sophisticates, the French. During the Reign of Terror in 1793–94, the victorious revolutionaries got so carried away with their self-righteous revenge that they slaughtered their countrymen by the thousands for crimes against the people, then for accusations about crimes against the people, then for the potential to engender accusations.

In Nantes the guillotine wasn't able to keep up with the volume of executions ordered by the tribunal. Condemned aristocrats, priests, government officials, and anyone else who ticked off the tribunal were crowded onto ships, which were then capsized in the river.

Any of the condemned who tried to escape drowning were pushed under the water with boat hooks.

The river became so littered with corpses that the contaminated water spread a fatal disease throughout the city. In their lust for vengeance, the revolutionaries accidentally killed themselves.

♕

Then there's the Russian Revolution.

In 1917 after successfully overthrowing the czar, the Bolsheviks agreed to a stupid peace treaty with Germany, which convinced Germany that Russians were fools.

The Bolsheviks were eager to stop fighting the Germans so they could rush home from the front and kill several hundred thousand of their own people in a civil war that prevented the country from solving its farming, manufacturing, and financial problems.

After winning the civil war, the Bolsheviks were in no condition to deal with famine, which killed millions more, and which led the Germans a decade later to assume that the Russians were still fools and could be conquered during World War II.

The Russians may have been fools, but so were the Germans, who ignored the lessons of Russian winters and Napoleon's ill-fated attempt to conquer Russia, and the willingness of Russians to die fighting any enemy under the fatalistic theory that they were bound to die fighting one enemy or another, or each other, so what's the difference?

None of the stupid excesses of the power-mad Communists during these thirty years of slaughter—the civil wars, the famines, the collapse of Russian industry, or the German invasion—slowed Joseph Stalin as he murdered millions of his own people, which at least prevented them from dying of starvation or German bullets.

The American nation was founded on the concept of freedom and the inalienable rights of all people. Unless those people happened to be Africans.

Millions of people who were going about their own business lost their homes, their families, or their lives so that other people didn't have to pay for hired help.

The legacy of slavery still plagues America today in racism, crime, and poverty.

What would have happened if the Americans who promoted liberty had actually upheld their beliefs and never stolen the liberty of Africans? America would be a better place today, and so would Africa.

⚜

Back to more common forms of power madness: In 1976 the charismatic Rev. Jim Jones of the People's Temple explained to his devout followers that "if you love me as much as I love you, we must all die or be destroyed from the outside."

Over nine hundred people either committed suicide or were helped along the path of death by people more devout than they. Parents killed their own children in the name of God.

After the mass suicides, the religion was declared a cult.

⚜

Jack Anderson wielded power in Washington through his investigative newspaper column, but not as much power as he thought. After the shah of Iran was overthrown by revolutionaries, Anderson claimed that he had predicted in his column the shah's fall from power years earlier.

The only problem: When people checked Anderson's old columns, it turned out he had not made the prediction.

In the ninth century, Erigena was one of the few enlightened scholars. He argued quite reasonably that "reason and authority come alike from the one source of Divine Wisdom."

The Church didn't take kindly to such wild heresy and banned Erigena's writings. Four centuries later, they were still considered heresy, so Pope Honorious III had his work burned as "hereditary depravity."

An evangelist was fined $1,700 in Salisbury, England, for a stunt in which he went up in a motorized paraglider so he could preach from above the rooftops to sinners on the ground. "I thought that maybe if they heard this voice booming out from the sky, they would think it was God," he explained.

In the thirteenth century thousands of French children believed a shepherd boy who claimed to have seen a vision of Christ. The children followed their young leader on a crusade to liberate the Holy Land.

The children were put aboard ships owned by French merchants, promised a free journey to Jerusalem, then sold into slavery instead.

The Assyrians were the most cultured people of the ancient world: productive farmers, deft craftsmen who promoted the age of bronze tools, merchants and traders who traveled the known world.

All that changed during the thirteenth century B.C., when they became the terror of the Mideast, amassing huge armies and annihilating their enemies. Their specialty: blinding captives, thousands at a time, to prevent slave revolts.

The fact that blind men then made poor slaves with limited abilities was lost on the Assyrians, who are also now lost.

At the height of the Roman fascination with gladiators, contest preliminaries entertained the crowds with the slaughter of unarmed men hunted down by armed fighters. The victor's reward: His weapons were then taken from him, and he became the next victim.

Reform-minded religious leader Martin Luther preached the value of the common man before the eyes of God and attempted to attain relief for the poor from a corrupt religious power base.

Interpreting Martin Luther's message of enlightenment their own way, German peasants in 1524 revolted and slaughtered dozens of German aristocrats.

Martin Luther tried to explain to the rebellious peasants that "the duty of a Christian is to be patient, not to fight."

The peasants went about the German countryside patiently killing the rich, claiming to be doing God's will.

God had nothing to say about the matter when the German army caught up with them and slaughtered thousands of peasants until there were none left to revolt.

⚜

In the Dark Ages, when Christianity was battling to take control of heathen European tribes, witches and pagans were condemned and killed for partaking in hysterical rituals, during which they would become possessed by the devil and dance about in an uncontrollable passion for hours, sometimes stripping naked as the Evil Force had its way with them.

From the 1300s to as late as the 1800s in Europe and America, devout Christians would become possessed by the spirit of God and dance about in an uncontrollable passion for hours, sometimes stripping naked as the Lord had His way with them.

⚜

Among the Kwakiutl Indians, tribal power was determined by who destroyed more of his own possessions. Thus, the truly power mad not only burned all their tools, weapons, and household items, but burned down their own houses.

They were then left with the power of nothing.

⚜

The power happy don't always resort to violence. Sometimes they try to rule by law.

As the popularity of automobiles grew in the late 1800s, the Pennsylvania Farmers' Anti-Automobile Society drafted the following regulations: "In the event a horse refuses to pass a car on the road, the owner must take his car apart and conceal the parts in the bushes. Automobiles traveling on country roads at night must send up a rocket every mile, then wait ten minutes for the road to clear."

The Pennsylvania legislature did not put these rules into law, as you'll note by the rarity of people dismantling their cars in front of horses.

Chapter 11

Dumbing Down the Arts

Artists often have no more idea of what they're doing than the put-upon outsider who stares and wonders: Is that art? Am I supposed to like that? Or am I just too gaga to get it?

Who knows, who cares, of course.

A frustrated writer came up with a novel scheme to test the intelligence of book publishers. He retyped into manuscript form *The Painted Bird*, Jerzy Kosinski's award-winning novel, and submitted it, under his own name, to a dozen big publishers.

They all rejected the manuscript as not being worthy of publication, including the house that had actually published Kosinski's book.

Vincent van Gogh, now considered one of the greatest painters in history, was a failure in his own time. Art critics in the nineteenth century scorned his work; collectors ignored him.

Van Gogh sold exactly one painting during his life, although they now bring millions when collectors sell them to one another.

German composer Richard Wagner wore gloves whenever he conducted a work by Felix Mendelssohn. After the music was over, Wagner threw away the gloves.

Why? Mendelssohn was Jewish.

Turn-of-the-century entertainer Tony Minnock had one of the most bizarre talents ever seen on the stage: He could withstand pain.

His act consisted of having himself nailed to a cross, like Christ, while singing to the audience.

Theodore Geisel's first book was rejected by twenty-three New York publishers before one dared to print it. *And to Think that I Saw It on Mulberry Street* went on to sell millions of copies, as did the rest of Dr. Seuss's many books.

Dubliners, a collection of short stories by one of history's greatest writers, James Joyce, was rejected by twenty-two publishers before getting into print. The entire first edition was bought by a book hater, who burned every copy.

An eighteenth-century merchant, Timothy Dexter, wrote and published his autobiography. The book contained not a single mark of punctuation—except for the last page, which consisted of line after line of periods, commas, exclamation points, and question marks, with the instruction to readers that "they may peper and solt [the book] as they plese."

Spelling wasn't a big issue with Dexter either.

How many of these books would have become best-sellers if their authors had kept the less-than-inspired original titles?

Bar-B-Q (*The Postman Always Rings Twice*)
Ba! Ba! Black Sheep (*Gone with the Wind*)
The Old Leaven (*The Sun Also Rises*)
The Various Arms (*To Have and Have Not*)
Something Happened (*Of Mice and Men*)
A Jewish Patient Begins His Analysis (*Portnoy's Complaint*)
The Terror of the Monster (*Jaws*)

Artists often claim it's their work that matters, the song not the singer. Unfortunately, governments believe that noble lie too.

Auguste Rodin, France's great sculptor, was broke, starving, and freezing during the harsh winter of 1917. He asked the French government if he could live in the museum where his sculptures were housed.

Government officials turned down the artist's request, and he froze to death in an unheated garret. Rodin had donated many of those sculptures for free to his beloved country.

The French writer Guy de Maupassant liked sex more than writing. He was eventually admitted to a mental institution, where he would lick the floors and refuse to urinate. He died of syphilis at the age of forty-two.

English writer Thomas De Quincey (*Confessions of an English Opium Eater*) often set fire to his own hair while reading bedtime stories to his children. Somehow he lived to be seventy-four.

Before Ed Sullivan became famous as the wooden host of a Sunday TV show, he was a theater critic in the 1920s. In his first review, he suggested the playwright August Strindberg should rewrite the second act of his play *The Father*.

Sullivan missed one crucial fact: Strindberg had been dead for nearly a decade.

A critic for the *San Francisco Chronicle* wrote a scathing review of the San Francisco Ballet Company's performance, particularly damning the lead ballerina.

After the review was published, people who had attended the performance pointed out that the critic had not—or he would have known that the particular ballet he criticized was changed at the last minute and the particular ballerina he blasted never actually danced that night—good, bad, or otherwise.

The editor of the *Chicago Tribune* refused to admit that Henry Miller's risqué novel *Tropic of Cancer* had made the best-seller list. So he simply stopped printing the full list.

Instead, the *Tribune* printed a selective column called "Among the Best-Sellers."

🎞

Artist Cosimo Cavallaro created a work of installation art by renting a New York City hotel room for $100 a night and covering everything in it with melted cheese. Gruyère, mostly, with Swiss and other varieties thrown in as the muse directed.

While fans of melted-cheese art had this work take their breath away, its main function seemed to be providing writers with a string of cheese puns: "Cavallaro has created a muenster. The art was as gouda it could get."

🎞

Need a reason to read those little signs on the walls in museums? Here's one posted at the *Titanic* museum in Indian Orchard, Massachusetts: "These postcards were donated by Janet Ripin, on behalf of her great-uncle, George Rosenshine, who perished in the *Titanic* disaster and had been in a steamer trunk for many years."

🎞

Heinrich Heine, the nineteenth-century German poet, left everything he owned to his wife when he died, on one condition: She had to get remarried.

That way, Heine said, "There will be at least one man who will regret my death."

The great playwright George Bernard Shaw wrote some of the finest, most intelligent speeches in the English language. Unfortunately, he didn't know how to stop talking. When he was eighty-two, Shaw came out in favor of the Fascists, Mussolini and even Hitler.

When the artists and animators who made cartoons for Hollywood movie studios organized into a union in the 1930s, the labor bosses didn't know where to put them.

They initially made the animators part of the Brotherhood of Painters and Paperhangers.

In medieval times the Catholic Church banned women from the stage in order to protect their morals. But the Church still wanted operas sung and needed singers with high voices.

The Church and its medical advisers solved that problem by castrating young boys so their voices wouldn't change as they grew older. The castratos were then trained to sing the women's roles.

This practice continued into the nineteenth century.

Belgian musician Joseph Merlin built the first roller skates in 1760. To make a big impression upon the aristocracy, he wore the skates to a London gala.

Thinking the skates alone wouldn't be enough of a sensation, Merlin rolled into the ballroom playing his violin. Therefore, he had no hands free to stop himself, and he crashed into a mirror. He nearly died from his injuries.

In 1561 a book called *Missae ac Missalis Anatomia* was published, containing fifteen pages of errata. The whole book ran to only 172 pages of text, setting a world record that has yet to be beaten for abominable proofreading.

British censors crept in slow motion through John Ford's 1935 drama about the Irish Rebellion, *The Informer*, and cut out every reference to the IRA or the rebellion—129 cuts in all, making the film completely unintelligible when it was released in England.

Hadji Ali, an Egyptian stage performer, had a brief career in the 1930s as the "Amazing Regurgitator." He would swallow buttons, jewelry, coins, and goldfish, then selectively regurgitate them.

An Englishwoman impulsively kissed a painting in an art museum in 1977. It cost the museum $1,260 to remove her lipstick from the canvas.

"I only kissed it to cheer it up," the woman explained. "It looked so cold."

Are you more superstitious than actors? Almost impossible.

We all know that the preferred wish of good luck to an actor about to go onstage is "Break a leg," when the actual breaking of a leg would be rather bad luck.

Theater tradition also maintains that a cat adopted by a theater brings good luck, as do shoes that squeak when you make your entrance.

Bad luck stems from including a picture of an ostrich in a stage set, whistling in the theater, or repeating the last line of a play during rehearsal.

If you can avoid all that, your career may be set, although it would also help if you could act a little.

A Japanese artist constructed a portrait of the Mona Lisa entirely from toast in 1983.

In the 1600s in England anyone caught singing or playing music in a tavern was whipped and imprisoned.

These punishments weren't a critical judgment, but a belief among royalty that romantic ballads and songs of any kind were a subversive threat to their reign.

The brilliant cellist Yo-Yo Ma put his concert cello in the trunk of a taxi at a New York hotel, then left it behind in the cab when he arrived at the concert hall.

"I did something really stupid," Ma said. "I just forgot."

Ma's 266-year-old cello was valued at $2.5 million. Ma may have been incredibly absentminded, but he was also incredibly lucky. Police tracked down the taxi and found the cello in the trunk.

In the sixteenth century a musician invented the cat organ. Cats were placed in a resonant box, with their tails extending through holes in the bottom of the box. The musician then played the chorus by yanking their tails.

Chapter 12

Military Unintelligence

They also serve who only sit and send us to our senseless doom.

The history of military idiocy is a long one because in no other field of endeavor are the entrance requirements so low and the effort so exhaustive.

Yes, sir, General, we'd be happy to go on that impossible mission and die. After all, we may be soldiers, but we're also idiots.

How many millions of stalwart young men have thought: Is this really how I should be throwing away my life?

Unfortunately, the thought comes as they charge across some crowded plain or up a barren hill into the face of certain death, at the precise instant that some order-issuing general on a hillside to the rear thinks: Oops.

Maybe that wasn't such a great idea.

Oh well, too late now. Better luck in the next war, chaps.

As a race, we applaud courage precisely because it flies in the face of all intelligence.

It took great courage for French knights to charge into the rain of English arrows from the longbows at Agincourt. But what idiots.

A little less courage and a little more brain power might have led the French to alternate strategies. They might have circled the outnumbered English to neutralize their longbows, instead of charging en masse down a narrow vale directly into the flight of massed points, thereby presenting the enemy with their single chance for triumph.

The Duke of Wellington once said, "There's nothing on earth so stupid as a gallant officer."

Yet could Wellington's army, or any army, have won a single battle without such gallant stupidity? War depends on men willing to shut down their brains, which counsel survival, and charge onto the enemy pikes. Remarkably, such men are never in short supply.

The Charge of the Light Brigade in 1854: How gallant, how stupid, how British.

In the Crimean War, an idiot captain ordered the six hundred men in the British Light Brigade, armed only with swords, to attack an entrenched Russian force consisting of six battalions of riflemen, six divisions of cavalry, and thirty cannon.

The Light Brigade lost four hundred of its six hundred men in twenty-five minutes. But they were not defeated until Russian soldiers on the surrounding hills fired into the battle, killing as many of their own men as the enemy.

During the Revolutionary War, George Washington led the Continental Army to their first victory by surprising the British troops at the Battle of Trenton in New Jersey.

Washington shouldn't have been able to surprise anyone. A Loyalist spy trying to report Washington's plans wasn't allowed in to see the British commander because the colonel wouldn't be interrupted while playing cards.

When the desperate spy finally sent in a note explaining that the enemy was advancing for a sneak attack, the British colonel put the note in his pocket unread and continued to play cards. It was his deal.

The note was later found on the dead colonel's body after Washington's victory.

In 1628 the Swedish navy built its largest and most dangerous warship, with sixty-four guns mounted on two decks. The ship proved dangerous to its own crew because of its inept design, and sank in Stockholm Harbor as it was launched for its maiden voyage.

The French army invented a blast-resistant boot allowing soldiers to walk over mine fields. One problem: The boot was so heavy and hard to walk in that the soldiers would be shot down by snipers long before they were not blown up by mines.

The Roman emperor Valens wisely sent for reinforcements so they could wipe out invading Goths.

Valens must have been affronted by his own sensible strategy because before the reinforcements could arrive, he led his outnumbered troops in a charge against the enemy.

The Goths must have been shocked to see Valens charge, since they had remained stationary, making no threat against the Romans, who could have waited at their leisure for reinforcements.

Instead, Valens managed to achieve the slaughter of two-thirds of his own army, including himself.

✪

In Scotland William Wallace (the Braveheart portrayed in the movie by Mel Gibson) had his bravery greatly aided by English arrogance, that curious pride of stupidity.

In 1297 a superior English force, led by de Warrenne, planned to annihilate Wallace's ragged army, but first had to cross the river Forth. Warrenne chose for his crossing Stirling Bridge, even though the Scots could be seen waiting on the other side and the bridge was so narrow only two men could cross at a time.

A mile upstream lay an undefended ford, wide enough for thirty English soldiers to march across side by side.

The Scots waited patiently at Stirling until a third of the English army had crossed the narrow bridge, then slaughtered them. A small detachment of Scot spearmen were able to bottle up the bridge, preventing the rest of the superior English army from riding to the rescue.

Wallace was undoubtedly as brave as Mel Gibson portrayed him, but his bravery would have been of little historical note if de Warrenne had not been quite so insistently vainglorious.

✪

Most bad leaders make mistakes of aggression, but inactivity can be as stupid as hyperactivity.

Union general George McClellan prolonged the Civil War by his hesitancy to engage the enemy, even though his forces were far superior in number to the Confederates.

In the battle over Munson's Hill, McClellan declined to attack after evaluating the hill as too heavily fortified with Rebel cannon.

After the Southern troops escaped under cover of darkness, Union soldiers discovered that the cannon that turned back McClellan from certain victory were logs painted black.

The general's indecision through a lengthy campaign grew so frustrating that President Lincoln wrote him this letter before relieving McClellan of his lack of command: "If you don't want to use the army, I should like to borrow it for a while. Yours respectfully, A. Lincoln."

☻

"Military strategy consists in making one mistake less than the enemy," the military strategist Hans Delbruck said. That task is often made easier by the insistent stupidity of enemy leaders.

In the second Boer War, British commander Lt. Gen. Charles Warren lost the battle of Spion Kop because he spent twenty-six hours personally directing the forces committed to the vital mission of ferrying the general's personal baggage across the river.

By the time Warren successfully completed that campaign, Boer reinforcements had arrived and dug in. Warren committed his troops to the attack just in time to get them decimated. No reports on the casualties among Warren's luggage.

At the Battle of Loos in 1915, ten thousand inexperienced British troops were sent in a frontal charge against German positions.

The British commander lied to his own men, telling them they were being sent to pursue routed German defenders.

Instead, the British marched directly into entrenched German machine guns, which mowed down eight thousand of them. The British could not break through because their leaders had provided them with no tools to cut the barbed wire.

German casualties? None.

The Germans were so astounded by the slaughter that they did not fire upon the British survivors as they retreated.

⊛

This is not to imply that the Germans were necessarily smarter. After all, they lost World War I, which wasn't as inevitable as it now seems.

In fact, the German army was on the verge of capturing Paris when they took a detour into the French wine country. They proceeded to get so drunk that by the time they resumed the attack, French and American reinforcements were in place.

The Germans soon sobered up enough to surrender.

⊛

During World War I, Corporal Alvin York's company was nearly wiped out. A sharpshooter, York managed to gun down twenty-five German soldiers, one at a time, luring them from shelter with the mating calls he'd used hunting turkeys back home in the hills of Tennessee.

One German soldier after another grew curious about the strange sounds. "Every time one of them raised his head, I just touched him off," York said, explaining how he came to panic a German battalion into surrender and win himself a Medal of Honor.

😵

On the other side of World War I, a single German soldier captured a French fort.

The infantryman on a reconnaissance patrol stumbled through a tunnel that led him into Fort Douaumont, where the French troops had posted no guards.

The surprised German soldier locked the enemy inside their barracks and opened the gates to his company.

In the Battle of Verdan, in which the fort was retaken, the French army lost 100,000 men.

😵

At Crecy in 1346 the French army attacked a much smaller force of English troops, composed primarily of longbow men, who stopped the first wave of French infantry. Before these foot soldiers could find cover, French mounted knights attacked along the same route, blocking their retreat, which also blocked their advance.

Instead of clearing the way for the survivors of the first wave, the French knights attacked their own infantry, while the English longbows slaughtered both groups at their leisure.

In 1750 British general James Abercromby attacked the French at Ticonderoga in New York state, near the Canadian border. His army outnumbered the defenders five to one and could have defeated them with a flanking attack, or an artillery bombardment, or even a siege.

Instead, Abercromby managed to wrest defeat from certain victory by sending wave after wave of his unfortunate soldiers in direct attacks against the French middle, the only fortified position the French held.

When a detachment of British troops actually managed to reach the French fortifications, they could not assault the nine-foot-high breastworks because the British had forgotten to bring ladders along on the charge.

In the 1916 Battle of the Somme, British commander Lt. Gen. A. G. Hunter-Weston ordered a frontal assault on German forces, telling his officers that the German defense had been destroyed by an artillery bombardment—even though everyone could see plainly that the German fortifications were intact.

The British charged directly into the German machine guns, and twenty thousand of them were slain in the first thirty minutes of the futile attack.

During World War I, soldiers on the Allied side were supplied with grenades mounted on sticks. The idea was to reach back and hurl the grenade over the trench, using the stick to leverage the throw, like a lacrosse player throwing a ball downfield.

But the grenades were designed to explode on impact, and trenches weren't wide. Many Allied soldiers lost their lives when they reached back and banged the grenade end of the stick on the back side of the trench.

💀

Everything stupid that can happen in battle happened to the American forces in the war against Spain, fought in Cuba in 1898. The only reason the Americans won the war was that the Spanish side was even dumber.

First, the American army didn't have enough men or supplies. Being forced into the war too soon by rabble-rousing politicians, the army didn't have enough time to train new recruits.

They chose an inexperienced general to lead the expedition to Cuba. He chose the wrong port from which to embark. The port didn't have room for enough ships and had only one railroad track, so supplies and men backed up for miles trying to load.

The general also chose the wrong place to land in Cuba, at a port where there was no way to off-load horses. Soldiers forced their horses overboard. Many horses, being even dumber than their riders, swam the wrong way, out to sea, and drowned.

The initial assault was so badly managed that a small force of Spanish soldiers could have ended the war right there by preventing the landing. But the Spanish commander didn't bother to send that small force of soldiers, so the Americans landed clumsily but unopposed, which was about the only way they could have landed.

The war's most famous battle, for San Juan Hill, was

only famous because it was so badly planned, led, and fought that vast American courage, and a vast number of American lives, were required to win it.

American soldiers suffered through repeated blunders by their officers, whereas with a modest amount of intelligent leadership and planning they might have won the battle much more easily.

A few scenes from the fight will suffice to explain how the Americans, who outnumbered the Spanish sixteen to one, almost managed to lose what seemingly could not be lost:

1. The American commanders didn't bother to gather reconnaissance, so they had no idea of how many Spanish soldiers were dug into the hill, or which were the best approaches to take to capture it.

   Instead, they used a hot-air balloon for their only reconnaissance during the battle. While the officer in the balloon could provide little actual information to the commanders on the ground, the balloon did serve one functional purpose—unfortunately, for the enemy.

   The balloon had to hover above the American troops so the observer inside could shout his observations to officers below. The Spanish defenders simply poured artillery and rifle fire into the jungle below wherever the balloon went.

2. The American attack was led by a National Guard unit composed of inexperienced soldiers armed with outdated rifles that fired old-fashioned black powder. The puffs of powder from their own rifles marked them as targets for the Spanish soldiers,

who returned more accurate fire with more modern weapons.

This American regiment proved so ineffective that they had to lie down in the grass to allow other units to pass them by and attack.

3. When the Americans reached Spain's first line of defense, barbed wire, they found that no one had brought wire cutters. Also, no one had provided for artillery support.

Unable to break through the wire, American troops had to hide in the jungle vegetation. When a battery of Gatling guns arrived, the American soldiers cheered. This gave away their positions, and the Spanish fired at the sounds, killing many men they couldn't see.

4. When the Americans finally started to advance up the hill, their artillery opened fire too late, hitting more Americans than Spanish.

5. All of this could easily have been avoided, since the Americans' naval guns could have forced the Spanish to abandon the hill or surrender. Only one problem with the naval guns: The Americans never used them.

The Americans did finally win the battle, at great cost, because the Spanish general was an equal match for the American general in terms of incompetence. He sent no reinforcements to a hill that could have been held.

Is it any wonder that German officers, in Cuba as observers, were not impressed with the American army, and didn't think it would be much of a fighting factor in wars to come in Europe?

After having failed to take the city of Syracuse by siege in 413 B.C., the Athenian army prepared to escape by sea before they were trapped by Spartan reinforcements.

As the Athenian soldiers started to board their ships, they came under the influence of a lunar eclipse. The Athenians disembarked, considering the eclipse a bad omen for sailing.

They were right in their reading of the omen, in a way, because the Spartan reinforcements arrived in time to block the harbor and kill 47,000 Athenians. The 7,000 survivors spent the rest of their miserable lives watching lunar eclipses as quarry slaves and wondering exactly how bad sailing away could have been.

In 1965 a U.S. Navy bomber dropped a practice bomb on a general store in Florida.

After two women officers in the U.S. Army were refused the Combat Infantryman's Badge for their actions in battle in the 1990 invasion of Panama, an army spokesman couldn't deny that the women had done their share in the fight.

Although women soldiers weren't allowed to go into battle, the battle had come to them. Displaying true army logic, he explained the denial of their medals this way: "We have a combat exclusion policy for women, but that doesn't mean women are excluded from combat."

Former Nazi general Sepp Dietrich complained in 1965 that Nazi veterans weren't being well treated, identifying them as a "persecuted community."

💀

The Vietnam War can be seen as folly on many levels. American soldiers who don't want to fight a war fighting for people who don't want them fighting it, kept there by American politicians who know the war can't be won the way it's being fought.

But we'll look at only one stupid aspect of the war because it is so modern in its foolishness: American soldiers were routinely sent to Vietnam for short tours of duty—one year at a time—in an effort by political leaders to prevent unrest among the GIs.

The stupid result: Just as American soldiers were learning to adapt to guerrilla war in the jungle, they were shipped home and new, jungle-ignorant troops were sent in.

In that way, the casualty rates among American soldiers were always kept higher than they had to be because experienced troops would have avoided many of the stupid deaths into which raw recruits stumbled.

Chapter 13

Stupid Science

For many dark centuries the dumbest science was: There was no science.

Anyone suggesting scientific investigation was branded a heretic and burned at the stake.

Science-deprived generations had to stagger along making a mess of the world in unscientific ways, believing that the universe was created by one of a variety of unknowable gods, rather than by one of a variety of unknowable theories of physics.

Now that our new and improved world is guided by a dominating science, we are no longer prey to the stupidities of ignorance. We are, instead, prey to the stupidities of science.

In 1971 Japanese scientists designed an experiment to study landslides. They watered-down a hill with fire hoses to create the effect of a massive rainstorm.

The hill collapsed. The resulting avalanche killed four scientists and eleven observers.

In an article on techniques for curing that dry mouth feeling, *Self* magazine had this scientifically proven advice for sufferers: "Take frequent sips of water."

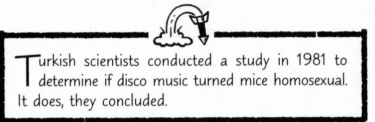

Turkish scientists conducted a study in 1981 to determine if disco music turned mice homosexual. It does, they concluded.

Scientists in Great Britain, who may have been colleagues of the researchers in Turkey, conducted a three-year study to determine whether fish feel pain when a fisherman gets them on the hook. Their conclusion: Fish do.

A grad student at Toronto's York University had his doctoral thesis, in which he analyzed the sociology of donut shops, approved.

In 1997 two Texas scientists built a six-foot, four-inch mousetrap. No six-foot mice have beaten a path to their trap.

In the 1600s English doctors prescribed tobacco as a cure for numerous diseases, including the plague.

In 1976 a swine flu scare swept through the United States. The government spent $135 million on a national vaccination program. Reacting badly to the vaccine, twenty-three people died, while hundreds of others had heart attacks or suffered paralysis. No swine flu was ever confirmed.

When DDT was created in 1939, its inventor received the Nobel Prize for developing an insecticide that would rid farms of mosquitoes and crop pests.

The Nobel Prize committee was as shortsighted as the inventor, who had failed to study DDT's long-term effects. Or perhaps they intended that the world should serve as their long-term study. DDT, they found out after enough sickness and death, was a worse solution than the problem.

In the 1970s a New York company packed twenty thousand tons of hazardous chemicals into leaking drums and buried them in a canal. A neighborhood was built on top of the canal, leading to birth defects and cancer for the little kids who lived there. The name of the dump: the Love Canal.

The United States Public Health Service conducted a thirty-eight-year study during which researchers told four hundred black men from Alabama that they were being treated for syphilis, even though they weren't.

The Health Service wanted to see what happened when syphilis victims were not treated. What happened? Many of the men died. All of them suffered.

No useful medical information was ever obtained. When the deceit was discovered, survivors and families of the victims received $9 million in settlement of a lawsuit against the government.

A Texas company will put your DNA samples on a rocket and shoot them into outer space. Why would you want to do that? According to the sales pitch: in case aliens are looking for human DNA to clone.

Scientists who tested and evaluated thalidomide decided it was such an effective sleeping pill that it could safely be sold over the counter without requiring prescriptions.

Somehow the scientists who developed the wonder drug missed the side effects. When taken by pregnant women, thalidomide caused horrible birth deformities, including babies born without arms and with flipperlike hands protruding from their shoulders.

Some eight thousand babies were born with these deformities before the drug was banned.

In 1984 in Bhopal, India, an insecticide plant storage tank containing methyl isocyanate sprung a leak, spewing poison gas over twenty-five square miles.

Even after the leak was discovered, it took two hours before the people of the town were warned of the danger. Two thousand of them died.

🐿

It took seven years to build the two-mile Tay Bridge in Scotland. The bridge was considered one of the great engineering marvels of its time, until it collapsed on December 18, 1879, during a storm eighteen months after it opened, sending a railroad train and eighty people to their death in the river below.

The people couldn't escape because the passenger cars on British trains were kept locked.

As for that engineering marvel, the engineer who had designed the bridge had failed to test for the effects of wind on the structure. He had also built it with inferior materials.

🐿

In 1963 cancer researchers at a Brooklyn hospital told twenty-three elderly patients they were going to take part in a new treatment program. Instead, they were injected with active cancer cells.

🐿

In the United States, the standard railroad gauge (the distance between the rails) is 4 feet, 8.5 inches. American track builders used that odd measurement because that's the way they built railroads in England. The

English engineers used the measure because the first rail lines were built by the same people who built the pre-railroad tramways.

Trams used that gauge because they were built with the same jigs and tools used for building wagons. The odd wheel spacing of wagons was designed to fit the wheels into the ruts of old English roads, which were carved into the dirt by Roman war chariots.

Civilizations may crumble, but specs never die.

✍

Military researchers came up with an ingenious plan to train bees to sniff out land mines on battlefields. The scientists reasoned that chemicals from the mines would be leached into surrounding flowers and then could be detected in the bee pollen.

The research was immediately opposed by animal-rights activists, who reasoned that bees should not be forced into military service, since they're not U.S. citizens.

Puts the K-9 corps into a new perspective.

✍

Dumb medicine can be practiced by patients as well as doctors. Take the case of a Belgian truck driver who thought he was following doctor's orders when he bought a bag of small nails at a hardware store. After dinner, the man swallowed several of the nails because his doctor had told him that he needed more iron in his diet. The metal cut into his stomach as he was rushed to the hospital.

In 1891 Isaac Cline, head of the U.S. Weather Bureau in Texas, told the Galveston newspaper that people shouldn't worry about hurricanes, even though the port city, which had been built only eight feet above sea level, had no seawall.

"It would be impossible for any cyclone to create a storm wave which could materially injure the city," the scientist asserted, further declaring that the concern expressed by other people was "simply an absurd delusion."

No defenses against storm or oceanic wildness were built. On September 8, 1900, a hurricane wiped out Galveston, killing eight thousand of its absurdly deluded citizens.

In the early days of rocket science, technicians were responsible for cleaning fuel tanks before test flights. Even small specks of dirt in a tank could alter the flight pattern and potentially destroy the rocket.

Before one launch, the technicians, dressed in clean suits, climbed down a ladder from the docking platform into the fuel tank and carefully cleaned the tank, eliminating every possible contaminant, wiping up every grain of dirt, every speck of dust.

When they returned to the control stations, remote instruments indicated there was still some contamination in the fuel tank.

So they reopened the hatch and pulled up the ladder.

TV minister Jerry Falwell announced in 1998 that computer pro-
gramming problems resulting from the Y2K bug "may be God's
instrument to shake this nation."

Falwell predicted that the problems of adjusting software to
recognize code for the year 2000 could start a worldwide religious
revival that would lead to Christ returning to take true believers
to Heaven.

In preparation for this long-awaited event, Falwell stocked up
on food and ammunition, although he did not make it clear why
he would need ammunition on the way to Heaven. Or food for
that matter.

⌂

Decades later, NASA spent only $125 million to send the
Mars Climate Orbiter 416 million miles to study the red
planet. Scientists, however, failed to spend a few bucks to
check their math.

One team of scientists responsible for navigation
used American measurements to calculate the orbit
around Mars. But the other navigation team used the
metric system. No one thought to make the conversion
between the two numbering systems.

As a result, before the spacecraft could go into orbit,
it crashed into the Mars surface and was destroyed.
Taxpayers can take comfort knowing that it was one of
NASA's inexpensive spaceships.

But it wasn't the first multi-million-dollar oops made
by our rocket scientists, who proved that sometimes
even rocket science isn't rocket science.

In 1962 *Marine 1* went off course and had to be

blown up before it crashed into the earth, at a cost of $18.5 million.

What went wrong? Someone put a hyphen in the wrong place in the directional computations.

🐑

When German university students took to saber duels in the eighteenth century, doctors had to stitch up their face wounds but not do a good job of it. Why did the injured students prefer bad stitching to competent repairs? Because the students were dueling for the scars. The more garish the scar, the higher a man's social standing.

🐑

Medical science during the Civil War lagged considerably behind military science. More than half of the 620,000 soldiers from the North and South who died in the war were killed not by bullets but by disease, or infections spread by army doctors.

One Union soldier wrote in a letter that, although wounded, he had refused treatment, thinking he had a better chance to survive on the battlefield than in the hospital.

🐑

Early European botanists called the eggplant "mala inana"—the mad apple—claiming that if you ate it—you'd go insane. Or maybe they were trying to convince their mothers that science said they didn't have to eat their vegetables.

An English doctor, James Salisbury, devised this unique cure for asthma in the 1880s: eating three, well-cooked beef patties a day with plenty of hot water.

The cure didn't work, but the hamburger-like entrée known as Salisbury steak stayed with us.

🦘

In prehistoric Europe, shamans attempted to cure epilepsy by cutting holes in the skulls of the sufferers. Such was their skill that people thus trepanned could survive the crude operations, and often returned for more treatments.

Oddly, trepanation made a startling return in 1962 when a Dutch doctor proclaimed that cutting away a small part of the skull would restore proper blood circulation to the brain, thereby raising consciousness.

The Dutch responded to this idea by putting the doctor in an insane asylum.

At least two of the doctor's English followers actually performed self-trepanation by drilling into their foreheads with electric drills and removing bone plugs from their craniums. Although neither had any medical training, they both survived the operations and opened an art gallery in London.

🦘

Ancient Romans didn't brush their teeth. Instead, following the advice of ancient Roman dentists, they prevented tooth decay by rinsing their mouths with urine.

🦘

The ancient Maori of New Zealand believed that God sneezed life into humans.

Taking the contrary view, many ancient European tribes believed that people could sneeze themselves to death by blowing the soul right out through the nose.

That's why we still say, "God bless you," when people sneeze, even though modern medical science does not suggest it as a preventive strategy.

🐑

In ancient Europe people were buried alive beneath the foundation of a castle or other major building because early engineers noticed that sometimes walls would shift and settle.

The engineers offered these people-bricks as sacrifices to gods of the earth to prevent the walls from crumbling.

Today's engineers prefer situation memos and team meetings as advanced techniques for ducking the blame.

In the Middle Ages doctors thought they could drive off a fever by putting a horse's head under a sick person's pillow. Probably the only way it drove off the fever was to drive off the sick person with it.

When scientists announced in 1954 that lung cancer among cigarette smokers was three to sixteen times higher than among nonsmokers, the number of smokers actually rose.

A Texas man suffered a fatal heart attack in 1995 when his pharmacist gave him high-blood-pressure medicine instead of an angina medication. The druggist couldn't read the handwriting on the doctor's prescription.

In the late 1800s, the English explorer Francis Galton turned his curious mind and considerable wealth to science, like his cousin Charles Darwin.

Among Galton's peculiar studies: a beauty map of Great Britain that he developed by counting the number of good-looking women he saw in each city (from London, pretty, to Aberdeen, ugly), the proper length of rope for hanging criminals, a pressure gauge for chair legs to determine to what degree people inclined toward their dinner companions, a quantitative evaluation of the dullness of lecturers, a sextant for measuring the figures of women from a distance, and his somewhat scandalous paper on the "statistical inquiries into the efficacy of prayer," which demonstrated, among other claims, that monarchs whose subjects pray for their long lives actually live shorter lives.

Galton was most infamous for promoting his science of eugenics, in which he proposed that only men from eminent families who exhibited the proper qualities of "health, energy, ability, manliness and courteous disposition" should be selected to form the breeding stock of England.

Idiots, criminals, and various other undesirables would be kept in labor camps and prohibited from breeding.

Another controversial geneticist, William Shockley, believed that his own children represented a "significant regression" in evolutionary intelligence from their father.

How had the Shockleys slipped? He blamed it on his wife's lack of high academic achievement.

🐾

Doctors in the nineteenth century locked patients inside a fever cabinet, in which high-intensity lightbulbs drove their temperature as high as 105 degrees, in an attempt to cure syphilis.

🐾

A British doctor devised the leech storm-warning system in 1851. His weather-analysis device consisted of a jar filled with leeches and a bell. When a storm approached, he predicted, the leeches would turn active, ringing the bell.

The doctor's idea was to establish a series of leech warning stations along Britain's coast. The government turned down the deal.

Chapter 14

Dumb Things Famous People Said

If you want to be famous, start early with mouth-stretching calisthenics so that by the time reporters start writing down what you say, you'll be able to get the whole foot inside.

In the race to sound really dumb, the politicians may have an insurmountable lead.

President Calvin Coolidge: "When more and more people are thrown out of work, unemployment results."

Ronald Reagan, when asked what qualified him to be president: "I'm not smart enough to lie."

Marion Barry, Washington, D.C., mayor: "Outside of the killings, we have one of the lowest crime rates."

President George Bush: "I have opinions of my own, strong opinions, but I don't always agree with them."

Vice President Dan Quayle: "What a waste it is to lose one's mind. Or to not have a mind. How true that is."

President Warren Harding: "Progression is not proclamation nor palaver. It is not pretense nor play on prejudice. It is not personal pronouns, nor perennial pronouncement. It is not the perturbation of a people passion-wrought, nor a promise proposed."

Ronald Reagan, opposing legislation to protect our national forests: "A tree's a tree. How many do you need to look at?"

Chicago mayor Richard Daley: "Get this thing straight once and for all. The policeman isn't there to create disorder. The policeman is there to preserve disorder."

Senator Barry Goldwater while running for president in 1964: "Many Americans don't like the simple things. That's what they have against we conservatives."

President Eisenhower's adviser Howard Pyle: "The right to suffer is one of the joys of a free economy."

Senator William Smith, chairman of the government committee investigating the *Titanic* disaster: "Why didn't the passengers on the boat go into the watertight compartments and save themselves from drowning?"

Senator Smith missed the obvious: Anyone who took refuge in the supposedly watertight compartments would have either suffocated or drowned when the ship sank to the bottom of the North Atlantic.

Vice President Dan Quayle again: "It isn't pollution that's harming the environment. It's the impurities in our air and water that are doing it."

Governor Alf Landon on the campaign trail against FDR: "Wherever I have gone in this country, I have found Americans."

Senator Orrin Hatch: "Capital punishment is our society's recognition of the sanctity of human life."

Geography knows no boundaries when it comes to political foolishness, as French president Charles de Gaulle demonstrated: "China is a big country, inhabited by many Chinese."

Once more from Vice President Dan Quayle: "I love California. I practically grew up in Phoenix."

Ron Ziegler, President Nixon's spokesman, explained a common political paradox this way: "The president is aware of what is going on. That's not to say something is going on."

But the politicians have no monopoly on the phenomenon of people who can talk without requiring the use of a brain:

Wealthy philanthropist George Delacorte gave his money generously to benefit New York's Central Park. But he refused to give anything to fight poverty, explaining that "people are poor because they're dumb or because they're lazy. If you feed them, you just keep them in the same strata."

Miss Alabama of 1994, answering one of the questions in the Miss USA contest: "I would not live forever because we should not live forever, because if we were supposed to live forever, then we would live forever, but we cannot live forever, which is why I would not live forever."

Actually, she made a lot of sense compared to the others.

NBC executive Warren Littlefield about deleting discussion of orgasms from the TV show *Sisters:* "Corporately, we believe in orgasms."

Mort Naham, producer of the short-lived TV show *The Secret Diary of Desmond Pfeiffer:* "Although they were potentially painful and difficult periods in history, they were ripe for comedy."

The show was about slaves suffering in the American South. It was a sitcom.

Talk show host Phil Donahue: "I'd rather be called sleazy than to be identified as intelligent."

Violinist Zubin Mehta: "I don't think women should be in an orchestra. They become men. Men treat them as equals. . . . I think it's terrible."

Financier Ivan Boesky: "I think greed is healthy. You can be greedy and still feel good about yourself."

Wealthy industrialist John D. Rockefeller: "I believe that the power to make money is a gift from God."

Supermodel Beverly Johnson made this unique plea for everyone to join in the battle against poverty, no matter what Rockefeller and Boesky thought: "Everyone should have enough money to get plastic surgery."

Actress Brooke Shields offered this zen view on cigarettes: "Smoking kills. If you're killed, you've lost a very important part of your life."

Actor Telly Savalas evaluated who in history was the villain of villains: "A man worse than Hitler or Stalin, I'm speaking of Sigmund Freud."

Multimillionaire basketball star Shaquille O'Neal, when asked if he visited the Parthenon while in Greece: "I can't really remember the names of the clubs we went to."

Oakland A's owner Charlie Finley on the baseball commissioner in 1981: "I've often called Bowie Kuhn a village idiot. I apologize to all the village idiots of America. He's a national idiot."

National Hockey League president Clarence Campbell in 1974: "There has never been any violence in the NHL."

✐

A happily anonymous book editor rejecting George Orwell's classic parable *Animal Farm:* "It is impossible to sell animal stories in the USA."

✐

Writers often save their dumbest thoughts for each other.

Virginia Woolf described James Joyce's labyrinthine novels as "the work of a queasy undergraduate scratching his pimples."

Joyce's master scratch, *Ulysses,* was declared the best book of all time by a panel of scholars in 1998. None of Woolf's writings were on the list.

Leo Tolstoy evaluated the work of William Shakespeare this way: "Crude, immoral, vulgar and senseless."

Yes, but did he like it?

Chapter 15

Idiotic Politics

"**S**uppose you were an idiot," Mark Twain ventured, "and suppose you were a member of Congress. But I repeat myself."

The connection between politics and stupidity is obvious to anyone who can bear to read the daily newspaper.

It makes you wonder: If politicians are so stupid, how do they ever get elected? Or does that answer the question?

Some politicians, by dint of working harder than others, manage to sink lower into the dumbing grounds of history.

While on a trip to Europe financed by taxpayers' money, Congressman Adam Clayton Powell studied work opportunities for American women in 1962 by visiting nightclubs and strip shows (all places American women could work).

Powell also charged taxpayers for his laundry, which he had cleaned in London and flown to Italy via diplomatic courier.

In 1971 Alabama governor George Wallace was awarded an honorary degree in the martial art of tae kwon do. You can't get an honorary degree in a martial art—fighting takes practice.

To save money, Congressman James Jeffords from Vermont moved out of his Washington, D.C., apartment and into his Capitol office. Congressmen in 1981 earned more than $60,000 a year.

Samuel Ferdinand-Lop ran for the presidency of France in the 1940s on the Lopeotherapy platform, which called for the elimination of poverty after ten o'clock at night and a unique way of improving the air in Paris: by relocating the city to the country.

More than 46,000 voters wrote in Edward Kennedy's name for U.S. senator in 1962. What's so dumb about that? These voters lived in Connecticut, while Kennedy was running in Massachusetts.

When the camp TV show *Batman* became popular in 1966, the Soviet government newspaper, *Pravda*, called the caped hero "a capitalist murderer." *Pravda* apparently preferred the more proletariat Joker and Riddler.

William Henry Harrison, elected to the presidency in 1840, wasn't stupid because he refused to wear a hat or coat to his outdoor inauguration in the middle of a March storm in Washington.

He was stupid because he was so in love with the sound of his own voice that he ran his speech for over an hour while everyone froze, including him.

Harrison droned himself into a serious head cold, which led to fatal pneumonia after only a month in office, making Harrison the first president to talk himself to death.

Hubert Humphrey wanted to be president so much that he agreed to serve as vice president under Lyndon Johnson. This was like a man who wants to learn to craft leather taking an apprenticeship with the Marquis de Sade.

As a politician, Johnson was an egotistical sadist who belittled Humphrey at every opportunity, once kicking him in the shins when the vice president didn't move fast enough to fulfill his boss's request.

"When I want your advice," Johnson told Humphrey, "I'll give it to you."

Despite his ignominy, Humphrey never got to be president. He lost the election to a politician who suffered even greater humiliations to get the job: Richard Nixon.

Harold Carswell, President Nixon's nominee to the Supreme Court, faced strong opposition. Democrats claimed that Carswell was not a distinguished enough judge to sit on the nation's highest court.

Senator Roman Hruska rose to a novel defense of Carswell's nomination.

"Even if he were mediocre," Hruska argued, "there

are a lot of mediocre judges and people and lawyers. They are entitled to a little representation, aren't they, and a little chance? We can't have all Brandeises and Frankfurters and Cardozos and stuff like that there."

Soviet dictator Joseph Stalin, whose reign of terror gave him the distinction of having killed more of his own people than rival megalomaniac Adolf Hitler, kept an entire nation in constant fear, wondering whom he would exterminate next.

Stalin once set the record straight by pointing out that "gaiety is the most outstanding feature of the Soviet Union."

General Joao Figueiredo, after being elected president of Brazil in 1979, showed an immediate flair for power politics.

"I intend to open this country up to democracy," he happily proclaimed, "and anyone who is against that, I will jail, I will crush."

In 1844 the Whigs ran against an obscure compromise candidate put forth for the presidency by the Democrats, with the insulting campaign slogan, "Who the hell is James K. Polk?"

Turns out Polk was the guy who beat the Whigs. Polk further distinguished himself by becoming one of the few, if not the only, presidents to fulfill every campaign promise he'd made. During his only term in office, these included winning the Mexican War and securing the Pacific Northwest for the United States.

As for Polk's taunting opponents, ask most students today and they'd answer, "Who the hell are the Whigs?"

Political expert Niccolo Machiavelli plotted a strategy for political affiliations in the afterlife that exposed the hypocrisy of most politicians.

"I desire to go to hell and not to heaven," he proclaimed. "In the former place I shall enjoy the company of popes, kings and princes, while in the latter are only beggars, monks and apostles."

President Richard Nixon held a White House dinner to honor jazz great Duke Ellington, then mistook singer Cab Calloway for the guest of honor, saying, "Pat and I just love your music."

Caligula, emperor of Rome, was so bloodthirsty that his own guards had to assassinate him to protect themselves from being next on his list.

In his lust for power, Caligula tortured and killed enemies and friends alike. He referred to Rome, whose people had made him emperor, as "the city of necks waiting for me to chop them."

President Ronald Reagan preached a great game of conservative economics, but didn't necessarily practice thrift when it came to spending money on what he wanted to spend money on. As an actor, Reagan knew that what you did could be covered up by what you said.

For his inauguration, Reagan spent more taxpayer money

than any president before him—at least $4 million by conservative estimates. How did Reagan defend his liberal spending policies? He simply proclaimed that no public funds were being used.

Such was his popularity that people believed him instead of the facts. Self-deluding responses encourage politicians to think they can fool the public enough of the time to have profitable careers.

When Warren Austin represented the United States in the United Nations in 1948, he offered a novel approach to settling problems in the Middle East, suggesting that Jews and Arabs settle their differences "like good Christians."

Richard Nixon's spokesman Ron Ziegler shed light on the president's position on the Watergate cover-up this way: "If my answers sound confusing, I think they are confusing because the questions are confusing and the situation is confusing and I'm not in a position to clarify it."

In 1998 a senatorial candidate from Oklahoma died a month before the primary election but still received 56,000 votes.

Maybe the electorate figured that a dead politician couldn't be any worse than a live one.

J. Edgar Hoover had FBI agents maintain a subversive file on poet Archibald MacLeish, who won the Pulitzer Prize three times and was Librarian of Congress.

What did Hoover come up with against the poet? Prior to World War II, MacLeish was "prematurely anti-Fascist."

Researchers tell us that nearly twice as many liberals as conservatives have gone skinny-dipping in their lives. Are liberals more daring? More prone to illegal activities? Or do they simply have better bodies?

Or perhaps conservatives lead equally wild private lives but keep them private by covering up their great, skinny-dipping bodies and not answering stupid questions asked by researchers.

Five-term congressman Sam Steiger of Arizona returned to politics after being out of public office for twenty-three years when he was elected mayor of the rustic town of Prescott in 1999.

Steiger grouchily accepted his victory, stating that the most interesting thing about the election was "that there were 96 people here stupid enough to vote" for his opponent.

How did it feel to be back in public office after such a long retirement? "It sucks," he explained.

President Gerald Ford declared that Poland was not under Soviet control in 1976, which must have come as a surprise not only to the Poles but also to the Soviets who controlled Poland at that time and had for many years.

To prove that there was no prejudice in the U.S. Army, President Ronald Reagan loved to tell the story about the black cook who shot down a Japanese Zero at Pearl Harbor. The only problem with Reagan's story is that it never happened.

Ironically, the U.S. Army was more integrated at the time than the rest of American society.

As for Reagan, he also campaigned against proposals for environmental protection by asserting that trees cause air pollution, which posed a threat to the nation's air quality because, according to Reagan, we had more forests in America now than in colonial times.

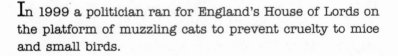

In 1927 incumbent president Charles King won the Liberian election with 234,000 more votes than his rival, which was odd because that was fifteen times the number of people who had voted.

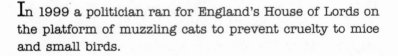

George Washington's enduring popularity is fostered among schoolchildren by the tales of his chopping down a cherry tree but telling his father the truth because he could not tell a lie, and of throwing a silver dollar across the Potomac River.

While the stories have been made to serve educational purposes for years, they're lies, made up by biographer Mason Locke Weems in 1800 to sell more books.

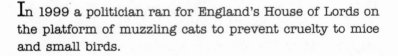

In 1999 a politician ran for England's House of Lords on the platform of muzzling cats to prevent cruelty to mice and small birds.

Chapter 16

Stupid Sports

They don't call them dumb jocks for nothing.

When Richard Nixon played football for Whittier College, he foreshadowed his approach to the presidency by being offside on nearly every play. There was only one thing the coach could do with his overeager player: bench Nixon.

The first four finishers of the 1900 Olympic marathon were disqualified for cheating. They left the race early, took a horse and carriage around the race path, and ran into the stadium ahead of the other runners.

The cheaters were easily found out because the real first-place winner had taken the lead early in the race, so he knew no one had passed him.

In basketball, power forwards are a breed unto themselves, which is probably just as well.

Utah Jazz power forward Karl Malone came up with this unshakable defense for the game's biggest showboat and fellow board monster, "Say what you will about Charles Barkley, when he tells you he is going to do something he'll either do it or he won't do it."

In 1998 Mark McGwire shattered the home run records of both Babe Ruth and Roger Maris, the greatest of the old, long-standing records. Even though McGwire didn't inch past the records but bombed them by hitting seventy homers, a sportswriter for the *New York Post* put the slugger down in seventh place in the ballot for most valuable player.

If you think football is rough now, ninety-five years ago it was played without helmets. Punching, kicking, and gouging were legal moves. During the 1905 college season, eighteen players were killed on the field.

Then there were the rules of a lacrosselike game played by the ancient Aztec and Maya Indians of Central America. The captain of the losing team was killed and his heart passed around among spectators for consumption.

When athletes make boneheaded plays, no one is particularly surprised that people nicknamed Daffy and Dizzy aren't always playing with a full helmet. But we expect an intelligent effort from the referees.

Track and field officials at the 1932 Olympics in Los Angeles set a world record for untracked minds. When Jules Noel of France broke the Olympic discus record, his winning throw was disqualified—not because of any infraction of the rules, but because all the judges who were supposed to be watching the discus competition had turned around to watch the pole vault instead.

During the 1972 Olympics, the United States basketball team won the gold medal in the final game against Russia. The horn sounded ending the game with the U.S. team ahead by a point.

Then an official overruled the clock, and gave the ball back to the Russian team. The Russians failed to make a basket, and time ran out again.

A second official overruled the clock again, and gave the Russians the ball again. This time they scored and were awarded the gold medal. The U.S. team boycotted the awards and their silver medals.

That incident remains the biggest blotch on the spirit of fair play, which the Olympics allegedly exemplifies, worse than athletes who use performance-enhancing drugs, worse than skating and gymnastics officials who favor certain competitions with subjectively high scores. Everyone saw the basketball officials make the wrong calls, not once but twice, until they got the result they wanted. No Olympics authorities responded to the protests.

At the Canadian rodeo in Edmonton, the game of cowboy poker became popular after being borrowed from a penitentiary rodeo event.

Four men sit at a table in the middle of the arena. They don't have to play cards and they don't need chips because they're gambling with their bodies.

The promoters select a nasty bull, who's let loose in the arena. When the bull charges the table, the last cowboy left sitting wins.

In November 1998, a bull smashed the poker table to shards, but the pot of $300 had to be split because two cowboys were still sitting there after the bull's charge.

Who says football stars don't make intelligent commentators on their sport? Consider this from ex-quarterback and TV expert Joe Theismann: "Nobody in football should be called a genius. A genius is a guy like Norman Einstein."

In the fashion of '90s athletes who use their bodies as posters, a USC tailback honored his mother by having her name tattooed across his chest.

He must have had a USC reverse on his mind, because he had her name tattooed Mabel, while Mom spelled it Mable.

Sports movies often look silly to sports fans because the actors are unconvincing as athletes. Most actors who start young in show business have no chance to play sports growing up; they're too busy going to rehearsals to try out for the team. So when they step up to the plate, they look like they've never swung at a live pitch before.

Then there was comic actor John Goodman convincing no one as the great Babe Ruth in the misguided baseball movie *The Babe*. Even worse than the actor was the writer, who had the Babe scoring an inside-the-park home run on an infield pop-up.

Something about facing a charging bull brings out the dumb ingenuity in certain matadors, including the man who tried to fight a bull from the back of a convertible Peugeot in 1901. Luckily, the bull didn't know it was a Peugeot, or he would have tossed the car.

Instead, the bull turned tail and ran, leaving the matador without a fight but a convenient way to beat his own hasty retreat from an arena filled with disappointed fans.

In 1897 a matador fought a bull from a bicycle. The bull was unimpressed, tossing man and bike over the wall. A bout between a bull and a matador on a motorcycle in Spain in 1932 ended in a draw, although not with the crowd, who showed enough disfavor that it wasn't tried again.

Ice brought out almost as many foolish athletes as bulls, including teams that played ice baseball in the late 1800s, a game in which sliding was not only allowed but unavoidable.

Other game athletes tried basketball on ice skates, while ice boxing had a flair of popularity in Cleveland at the turn of the century.

If they weren't sliding all over the ice, athletes were falling from their mounts as they tried football, boxing, and basketball while riding horses.

In the short-lived sport of water baseball, regulations required that infielders stand in the water up to their necks, the pitcher up to his waist, and the batter up to his thighs.

Other short-lived sports that required a certain adroitness but little brainpower: aerial golf, flagpole sitting, and goldfish swallowing.

In 1878 long-distance race walker Lyman Potter offered a $1,500 challenge to anyone who could push a wheelbarrow from San Francisco to New York faster than he could.

Amazingly, Potter's challenge was taken up by Leon Federmeyer, a forty-one-year-old French wheelbarrow pusher.

Loaded down with 133 pounds of food, clothes, and a tent, Federmeyer pushed that wheelbarrow across the desert, through winter storms, and over the mountains.

Six months later, Federmeyer shoved that wheelbarrow into New York City to claim the championship. His opponent—and the prize money—never showed up.

A broken Federmeyer tried to recoup by entering other long-distance walking (although wheelbarrowless) contests. Oddly, he raced slower without a wheelbarrow than he did with one.

Boxing hit a pre–Mike Tyson low when heavyweight great Muhammad Ali accepted a challenge bout for the "martial arts championship" of the world from Japanese wrestler Antonio Inoki.

Ali took care of the prefight publicity, while Inoki performed special martial arts training to strengthen his chin to withstand Ali's bee-stinging fists.

Inoki needn't have bothered with all the chin work. During fifteen rounds of attempting to prove that boxing didn't have to be a contact sport, he spent the match lying on his back, kicking at Ali anytime the boxer came near. Judges called the fight a draw.

The wrestler vs. boxer controversy was finally settled (or at least the huge wrestler vs. mediocre boxer controversy was settled) in 1976 when seven-foot-four wrestler Andre the Giant picked up journeyman boxer Chuck Wepner and tossed him out of the ring. Wepner stayed out, and Andre won, although both sports lost.

In the 1920s the Salem Trade School had the longest losing streak of any high-school football team in Massachusetts. After Salem played six years of losing football, league authorities discovered that there was no such school.

The team was composed of school dropouts who booked games with schools around the state for a share of the gate. The Salem eleven then made sure they lost so they'd be invited back again next year.

The ancient Minoans practiced a sport that defies modern athletes, at least those hoping to remain athletes for another day.

A young man or young woman would stand in the middle of an arena and face a charging bull. When the bull got close enough, the athlete had to grab the bull by the horns and somersault over the bull's back.

This sport may be one reason why there are so few Minoans left today.

🎆

Tennis player Ilie Nastase set a record for dumb behavior, pro division. During various matches, he mooned a referee, spat at an opponent, forfeited after his opponent charged the net and attacked him for his behavior, and was disqualified during a match in which his opponent was leading but walked off the court in disgust because of Nastase's inclination to do everything but play tennis.

🎆

In 1995 a man in India balanced on one foot for seventy-one hours and forty minutes. Foot-balancing is not a major money sport.

Other sportingly dumb attempts to get into the *Guiness Book of World Records* by people with more brawn than brains include:

1. A man in England who balanced one hundred bricks (weighing forty pounds) on his head for fourteen seconds.
2. A man who used his tongue to tie 833 cherry-stem knots in one hour.
3. Two men from Scotland who set the record for crawling (voluntary division) 31.5 miles on all fours.

That was the sprint event. For long-distance crawling, we look again to India where a man crawled 870 miles over fifteen months to demonstrate his religious devotion.

4. A British man who sliced a 12-inch cucumber into 264 slices in 13.4 seconds.

5. It took one of America's most prestigious universities to produce this mind-number: fourteen Stanford students who spent 244 hours and 43 minutes playing leapfrog. They covered 996 miles.

6. A Brit who walked seventy-two miles in twenty-five hours balancing a milk bottle on his head.

7. An American who rode a unicycle fifty-three miles and three hundred yards backward, looking over his shoulder the entire time.

In the 1976 Olympics, a Soviet army major competing in fencing, the sport of gentlemen, was disqualified for rigging his sword with a circuit breaker so he could register a hit on an opponent without actually making a hit.

King James IV banned golf from Scotland in 1491 for the simple noble reason that "it looketh like a silly game."

Later the king took up the game, and the law was changed so that golf was banned only on the Sabbath during the "tyme of sermons."

In 1967 K. V. Switzer became the first woman to run in the Boston Marathon. At least she ran until a race official tried to drag her off the course. Another runner stopped him.

After the race, Switzer was suspended from AAU competition for running longer than the 1½ miles permitted women and for running a marathon without a chaperone.

Thousands of women now compete in long-distance races annually, chaperoning themselves.

When it comes to team owners, George Steinbrenner of the New York Yankees is in a class by himself, primarily because no one else wants to be in that class.

After playing revolving doors with a series of managers, he announced in 1982 that "Bob Lemon is going to be our manager all year. You can bet on it. I don't care if we come in last. I swear on my heart he'll be the manager all season."

Steinbrenner then fired Lemon after fourteen games.

In the old days of bare-knuckle boxing, the rounds weren't timed. A round would last until one of the boxers was knocked down.

An 1871 bout between Jem Mace and Joe Coburn demonstrated the weakness of that rule. At the bell for the first round, the slugging Mace took up his stance in the center of the ring. But Coburn, a superior boxer, danced along the ropes. Neither man would alter his strategy.

The first round dragged on for seventy minutes without a punch being thrown, at which time police came and broke up the illegal fight, although how it could legally be classified as a fight no one could explain.

In 1912 a team of college all-stars played a football game against Gallaudet College, whose students were all deaf or hearing impaired.

The all-stars assumed that none of the opposing players could hear them, so instead of huddling to call a play they simply shouted out all their plays at the line of scrimmage.

The all-stars didn't realize that all of the Gallaudet players were expert at lipreading. Knowing every play the all-stars were going to run, Gallaudet blanked them 20–0.

Back before they had a shot clock in basketball, Illinois's Georgetown High School demonstrated why they needed one. After scoring a free throw early in the game, the Georgetown team stole the ball from their Homer High opponents, then stalled for the rest of the game.

Unable to break the freeze, the Homer players eventually sat down on the court, while the referee read the newspaper. When time ran out, Georgetown celebrated their 1–0 victory.

Chapter 17

Dumb Things You
Can Waste Your Money On

If we bought all the things the ad agencies told us we needed, we'd be as dumb as they think we are.

But who exactly are they marketing this stuff to?

Thunderwear: a groin pouch for holstering your gun. The manufacturer advises that on large-grip guns, you should wear pants with a skoosh more room in them.

For dangerous ladies, there's a gun holster that attaches to your bra.

A couch-potato snack bowl that emits a crowd roar every time you reach for the chips.

A clear plastic tube bracelet that you fill with ants, then wear around your wrist.

Aspirin earrings. The pill-mounted drop earrings also come in Valium, Sudafed, and Pepcid AC.

They sell all kinds of souvenirs at the Mount Rushmore gift shop. Our vote for the one that makes the least sense for tourists who have come to observe mountainous images of famous presidents: the $7.99 baseball with fake autographs from presidents George Washington, Thomas Jefferson, Abraham Lincoln, and Theodore Roosevelt.

Washington and Jefferson never even heard of baseballs, much less the concept of autographing them.

A gold-plated slinky for $129.95.

An inflatable rubber airplane.

An electric tongue cleaner.

A phone shield designed to prevent electromagnetic fields from seeping into your ears when you talk on the phone.

Air bags built into your underwear. The air bags deploy when you fall, to prevent hip injuries.

A sneezing doll.

A sneaker-shaped bed, under which you can put your bed-shaped sneakers.

Dog owners seem to be heavily identified by marketers as a target audience for all kinds of junk designed for consumers with their brains on a short leash.

How about edible greeting cards for dogs? Since your dog can read, maybe you should get him a book to go with the card, okay?

Or Rover might prefer a dog shampoo that smells like baby powder. Why baby powder? Because dogs have become the babies of the family.

Minivans with built-in TV sets. Just what drivers with car phones, car faxes, and satellite mapping systems need: something else to distract them from focusing on the road.

A souvenir A-bomb that goes off with a bang and a flash, and produces a mushroom-shaped cloud of smoke. It's made in Japan.

Rock 'n' roll pants that connect to a stereo system for good trouser vibrations.

Sparkling mineral water for plants.

T-shirts with fake sweat stains under the arms.

See-through underpants for men.

Psychic perfume blended to enhance your ESP abilities.

An executive door closer so busy CEOs can use a push button to hydraulically shut the office door in your face.

Chapter 18

The Business of Stupidity and Vice Versa

Hewlett-Packard once came up with the bright idea of removing all the doors from its offices to encourage open communication among management and staff.

Any time, any day, you could look out into the parking lot and see scores of people in twos and threes huddled among the cars, having the private conversations they couldn't have in their door-less offices.

But surely all corporations can't be run by people with their brains on permanent break time. Or can they?

Pacific Bell sent a multipage phone bill to customers even if they only had one page worth of charges. Many light phone users received a second page of their bill upon which were printed only two words: *blank page*.

When the Gillette company started selling safety razors in 1902, men by the hundreds bought them, then threw them away, claiming the razors wouldn't shave their beards.

Gillette officials found out that the dissatisfied customers weren't removing the paper wrappings before shaving with the blades.

🖼

Car companies spend millions researching the names for new models. Chevrolet came up with Nova, then found they couldn't sell it in Latin America because *no va* in Spanish means "doesn't go."

🖼

You know how hard it can be to find what you're looking for in a big department store, especially if you've never been there before. Perhaps that's why a California store posted this sign: SECOND FLOOR: UPSTAIRS.

🖼

British Rail was having trouble keeping its InterCity express trains running on time in 1998, but executives solved the problem without a major overhaul of equipment or systems enhancement.

They simply redefined "on time." Now trains run on time if they arrive within an hour of schedule.

🖼

In 1990 an American was reading the operation manual for his new VCR and noticed that the date used as an example of how to set the VCR's timer was December 7.

The VCR was made by a Japanese manufacturer. December 7 was the date of the Japanese sneak attack on Pearl Harbor that triggered America's entrance into World War II.

A California consultant sold corporations on a team-work training program called Kindergarten for Grown-Ups, in which executives built forts and strung noodle necklaces.

At least this program worked. It made them better managers by keeping them out of their employees' hair for a day.

Once matches became the common way to light cigarettes, soldiers learned that it was not safe to share matches during wartime.

That's how the superstition against lighting three cigarettes on a match began. Hold a match in the darkness for that long and an enemy sniper has time to aim and fire, making it unlucky to be the third on a match.

Match manufacturers exploited that sensible precaution by turning it into an international superstition that had nothing to do with surviving a war.

The result: People wouldn't share matches in peacetime, when no snipers threatened them, which increased the number of matches used and the profits of match makers.

Mark Twain, who was about as smart as Americans get, had the chance to invest his money in Alexander Graham Bell's new telephone company. He turned down the offer and sunk his money in a new kind of typesetting machine. That company lost everything and declared bankruptcy.

An English shipping company paid $2 million in damages to South Pacific islanders in 1998 when its giant freighter destroyed the island's coral reef while maneuvering too close to shore.

Why did the ship venture out of the channel? The skipper wanted a closer look at the island's topless women.

The tasty, sweet crust of that Black Forest ham comes from caramel. Unless you're in Canada, where meat processors received government permission to replace the expensive caramel coating with rust. Rust, the experts say, is cheaper, sticks to the ham better than caramel, and is safe for human consumption.

A worker in an Alexandria, Virginia, company was unhappy with his annual job-performance rating. He called his manager to complain. Than he called again, and again.

After the fiftieth complaint, he was arrested for harassment, convicted, and sentenced to thirty days in the county lockup.

What was his complaint? He felt he should have been rated outstanding. What had his manager rated him? Highly successful.

Perhaps complaining is a trait of highly successful, but not outstanding, people.

For several months, nurses were baffled to find a patient dead in the same bed every Friday morning at a South African hospital.

There was no apparent cause for the death. An

extensive search for possible bacterial infection failed to reveal any clues.

Officials finally discovered that every Friday morning a cleaning lady would enter the ward, remove the plug that powered the patient's life support system, plug her floor polisher into the outlet, then wax the floor.

When she had finished her chores, she would plug the life support machine back in and leave, unaware that the patient was now dead.

🖼

A Ukrainian businessman, who had bought pagers as gifts for each member of his staff, was so alarmed when all fifty of them went off at the same instant that he drove his car into a lamppost. After he checked himself for injuries, he checked the messages on the fifty pagers. They all read: "Congratulations on a successful purchase!"

🖼

In 1997 you could spend $7 for a polo shirt from a discount mart, or you could buy a designer shirt for $49. *Consumer Reports* magazine tested both for durability and general workmanship. Guess which came out on top? Yep, the cheapie.

🖼

Japanese women were sold on Infidelity Detection Cream, an invisible gel they could spray on their husbands' clothes. If he disrobed during the day when he was supposed to be at work, the clothes would change color.

The most noticeable result of the promotion: More Japanese men started washing their own clothes.

A sign outside a secondhand shop: WE EXCHANGE ANY-THING—BICYCLES, WASHING MACHINES, ETC. WHY NOT BRING YOUR WIFE ALONG AND GET A WONDERFUL BARGAIN?

Message on a leaflet: "If you cannot read, this leaflet will tell you how to get lessons."

Spotted in a toilet in a London office: "Toilet out of order. Please use floor below."

After helping to disgrace the presidency by having an affair with a married president while interning at the White House, Monica Lewinsky tried to capitalize on her infamy by selling purses through the Internet, each one bearing the curious label: "Made especially for you by MONICA."

Ms. Lewinsky really wanted her own lipstick line. "I'd like to have a lipstick," she told *Marie Claire* magazine. "I think it could be a neat thing, something that would be fun and lucrative and a respectable decision. Um, I'd like to be using my head again."

How about the Emeryville, California, restaurant that changed its name from Bavarian Village to Sushi Village. What's dumb about that? It was a Chinese restaurant.

Keenly aware of the new businesswoman's need to save precious seconds in her day, *New Woman* magazine offered this suggestion: Save time by "seeing several friends at once."

Pennsylvania farmers in the nineteenth century weren't going to be easily hoodwinked when oil was discovered on their land and business tycoons offered them a percentage of the profits in exchange for drilling rights.

Some farmers rejected the oil company's offer of ½ the profits and held out for ¼ because 4 was larger than 2.

For thirty-two years, a dentist in northern China collected 28,000 diseased teeth that he had extracted from his patients' mouths.

What did he do with so many rotten teeth? He built a tower with them, eight feet four inches high, to raise awareness of dental hygiene.

The plague of the fourteenth century had one unexpected result: the birth of the workers' movement.

When France was faced with a labor shortage because the black death had claimed so many peasants, surviving peasants went on strike for workers' rights.

The French nobles responded in true management fashion: They massacred the strikers and tossed their bodies in the rivers with the plague victims.

The looting of the New World by adventurers from the Old was more of a business venture than a military campaign. It's just that Spanish conquistadors found it a sensible business practice to slaughter the natives of South America as a convenient way of investing in Aztec gold.

Occasionally, the Spanish businessmen had trouble organizing their transportation divisions.

In 1520 Cortés and six hundred of his business associates arrived in the Aztec capital of Tenochtitlán and proceeded to acquire vast amounts of gold and jewels through the trading practice known as killing the other party.

But the city was an island in a lake, with only one way off: a long series of bridges. When the Spanish tried to conclude their transaction and depart, Aztec warriors destroyed some of the bridges, then attacked in canoes from both sides.

The Spaniards could have escaped if they had brought boats or had dropped their loot and run for it. But weighed down by gold, half the Spanish investors were killed.

Fortunately for Cortés, the Aztecs killed so many gold-heavy Spaniards that their bodies falling into the lake formed a bridge that the rest could run across, and flee to invest again another day.

When coffee was introduced by Venetian traders working the Arab routes, it was banned by the Italian clergy as the drink of infidels, until Pope Clement VII had a cup. Suddenly, coffee wasn't so evil. He pronounced it a moral drink for Christians.

One of the Western world's first dictionaries, the *Manipulus Vocabulorum*, written in 1570, had a unique approach to helping people understand the meaning of words: Instead of listing words alphabetically, the authors arranged them by the spelling of the final syllable of each word.

In Venice, prostitutes in the sixteenth century took to wearing shoes so high they were more like low stilts. The government eventually made prostitutes' shoes illegal, not on moral grounds but because too many women were falling off their shoes.

When Sir Francis Drake returned to England in the late 1500s, he brought back his New World discovery: pipes and tobacco. When he lit a pipe to show Queen Elizabeth how to smoke, a royal servant threw a bucket of water on Sir Francis, assuming he was on fire.

The next time you're trying to help a smoker quit, you might want to try the Elizabethan approach.

In the 1630s Dutch farmers started speculating wildly in tulips, driving up the price of bulbs into the thousands of guilders.

The spiraling speculation eventually bankrupted thousands of Dutch businessmen when investors realized that tulips had no inherent value that made them worth so much money, a lesson today's baseball card and Beanie Baby collectors have yet to learn.

In the 1950s an engineer was asked by an electronics manufacturer to improve push-button tuners for radios so they wouldn't lose contact with the station and slip into static.

His solution called for buttons that you could pull and also turn to fine-tune the station. His idea was rejected—not because it didn't work (it did), but because the company didn't want their radios to look different from everyone else's, which all performed poorly using push buttons.

Consumers become so accustomed to having things a certain way that improvements often have to be abandoned or disguised.

Take the QWERTY keyboard, which was designed to slow down typists by putting the most frequently typed letters under control of the weakest left-hand fingers. The nineteenth-century machines weren't mechanically trustworthy enough to keep up with fast typists.

Now word processors can go much faster, but the old slow-down keyboard arrangement remains the same because no one wants to learn a new one.

The British manufacturer Ariel produced a superior design for their motorcycle by moving the fuel tank to the rear of the frame. Designers then had to add a fake tank up front because riders were uncomfortable without it, even though they didn't need it.

The Sydney, Australia, Opera House is one of the city's most recognized landmarks, with its flamboyant design evoking the images of sailboats.

That fantastical design ignored engineering realities, resulting in nine years of construction delays that ran up the budget 1,400 percent. Engineers still couldn't solve enough of the design problems to avoid a $75 million, ten-year rehab project only sixteen years later.

Tin cans were a marvelous invention in 1810, allowing the preservation and transportation of food far from its source—particularly useful for armies on the march.

The only problem: No one invented a can opener for forty-eight more years.

Until then, soldiers used knives and bayonets to open the tin cans—and if that didn't work, they shot them open.

One food manufacturer included these operating instructions on his tin cans: "Cut round on the top with a chisel and hammer."

When the Chevrolet Monza was first designed, you had to remove the entire engine just to replace two spark plugs.

When Ford was approached by one of its designers to produce the first minivan in the 1970s, the company not only turned him down, they fired him. He went over to Chrysler, which then cornered a market that no other car manufacturer thought existed.

IBM turned down the chance to manufacture the first office copiers in the 1960s because IBM execs thought there would be no market for them.

The Gerber company made a fortune selling baby food in tiny jars. But the company flopped big time in the 1970s when they tried to sell single-serving food for adults in the same baby food jars.

Among ancient Assyrian traders, no business deal was finalized until the seller gave the buyer a single shoe.

The exploration of remote and remotely understood territories was risky business. Choose intelligently and you could bring home the gold—or at least the corn and tobacco.

Then there was nineteenth-century English explorer John Franklin, whose crew of 129 ill-fated men did not come home at all.

As Franklin struggled through the vast icy regions of the Arctic territory, his men lugged along a clothes brush, a tin of button polish, a backgammon board, and books.

They neglected to bring along their rifles, which would have enabled them to shoot game along the way. Instead, they all starved to death.

When Hungarian millers developed a more efficient grinding process for turning wheat into flour in the 1850s, they discovered that the new mills removed the nutritious bran and germ from the wheat, leaving the bread flour white.

To solve their marketing problem, they promoted a campaign to convince people that the white bread made from devalued flour was better than whole wheat bread because white was the color of nobility.

Movie theater owners in the 1920s barred patrons from eating popcorn during the show, thus depriving themselves of vast profits. Once they switched positions, theater operators learned that they made more money off snacks than movie tickets.

Ice cream sales in Japan plummeted during World War II because people feared they would be identified as traitors if they ate the American novelty. What they didn't know was that ice cream was invented by Italians, Japan's allies during the war.

New Coke.

All right, that's too easy a slam. It's not a brainless mistake for Coke to try a new formula. But it was a soda blooper of economy-size proportions for a company to spend two years on research, taste tests, consumer awareness studies, and focus groups, and then come up with a yecchy pop that everyone immediately hated. That $4 million wasted on New Coke left a bad taste in plenty of mouths when it was introduced in 1985.

A decade later, the Coca-Cola company announced they were developing a soda vending machine that could sense changes in temperature so it could raise prices when the weather got hot and people got really thirsty.

Americans spend two billion hours mowing their grass each year. None of them enjoy the chore. All of them know they wouldn't be mowing it if they weren't growing it. Yet they never stop growing it, so they never stop mowing it. For this dubious privilege, Americans spend millions of dollars on seed and mowers, only to end up with lawns that don't look as good as their neighbors'.

When soda pop was invented in the 1880s, it was sold as a medicine. Now people who drink too much of it may have to take medicine to counter the calcium-depleting effects of soda.

On the Pacific island of Alor, natives developed a monetary system based on drums and gongs that were never played and were spent only to buy pigs and wives.

Among natives of the Admiralty Islands, dog teeth were the currency exchange for wives, while on the isle of Yap the currency took the shape of twelve-foot-tall carved stones that weighed over a ton, which at least prevented them from getting shortchanged.

In 1911 the *Ladies' Home Journal* fired fifteen women for the shocking transgression of dancing the turkey trot.

A tired mother, Marion Donovan, invented the disposable diaper in 1951 by cutting up a plastic shower curtain. When she tried to sell the idea to American manufacturers, they told her it would never become popular enough to make money.

When Bette Nesmith invented Liquid Paper to correct typing mistakes in the 1950s, manufacturers turned her product down, convinced no one would want it.

Forced to finance production herself, she made a fortune.

Cheap, disposable paper dresses enjoyed a brief fad in 1966, until women found out that the dresses fell apart in the rain and caught fire easily. They were also uncomfortable.

Out of a job but not out of ideas, adman Gary Dahl sold over a million Pet Rocks in 1975. A Pet Rock was a rock in a box. They made Dahl a millionaire.

Trying to cash in on the blue jeans craze in 1974, American Motors put out an edition of its Gremlin and Hornet upholstered in denim. The cars didn't sell. The company missed the essential idea: that people wanted to wear jeans, not drive in them.

 F our million women in the 1970s spent \$40 million on mail-order breast enlargers that didn't work.

🖼

 W hen airlines began commercial flights, passengers were not allowed to buckle their own seat belts. Stewardesses were required to buckle up each one of them.

🖼

 A n actual tip from a Silicon Valley electronics company's *Environmental, Health and Safety Handbook for Employees:* "Blink your eyelids periodically to lubricate your eyes."

🖼

 F rom the 1983 edition of the employee manual from Morgan Guaranty Trust Company: "Avoid saying hello. This elsewhere pleasant and familiar greeting is out of place in the business world."

🖼

 L et's end with just a few product-label instructions:
1. On Nytol sleep aid: "Warning: May cause drowsiness."
2. On a hairdryer: "Do not use while sleeping."
3. On Chinese-made Christmas lights: "For indoor or outdoor use only."
4. For a Rowenta iron: "Do not iron clothes on body."
5. On a pudding package: "Product will be hot after heating."
6. On a bag of Frito chips: "You could be a winner! No purchase necessary. Details inside."

Chapter 19

Advertising How Dumb We Are

Dumb advertising is an industry built upon a simple premise: They're smarter than we are.

Ad agencies think of consumers as fools who can be tricked into buying any swill they sell. If there's a truth that works, fine, advertise that. If not, lies will do the trick just as well.

That explains the old gasoline ad that showed Our Brand producing clean exhaust, while Their Brand produced black, sooty exhaust. Was Our Brand really a cleaner gasoline, good for your car and our mutual air? Or did the ad provocateurs simply use a car with a dirty motor for Their Brand of gas?

Oddly, this is not just the view of a cynical age. Decades ago, when advertising was a fledgling, uncertain influence on mob-buying persuasions, advertisers still took our forefathers, not to mention our foremothers, for idiots. Consider these ancient advertisements:

A 1910 ad for Gillette razors: "You don't have to take a correspondence course to learn how to use it. Just buy it and shave."

From a 1930 ad for Drano liquid cleaner: "I can feel his eyes accusing me every time the bathroom drains slow up. He'd look at me as much to say, 'Your fault!' And it was."

📖

From a 1918 ad for corsets: "Women play a most important role in the affairs of the world. It's not only their privilege to represent the highest type of beauty, it's their duty to do so."

📖

An ad for Lestoil household cleanser shows a pretty model in a space suit and the pitch: "Women of the future will make the moon a cleaner place to live."

📖

From a 1944 ad from the American Meat Institute: "Human nature's yen for that good meat flavor is one of the most consistent manifestations in the history of food."

📖

Who could resist this pitch for soda in 1962: "7UP stimulates your mouth's natural moisture"?

📖

In 1928 Lucky Strike sold cigarettes to women with aviator Amelia Earhart's endorsement through the intriguing slogan: "For a slender figure, reach for a Lucky instead of a sweet."

If you reach for enough of them, you could end up with a figure as slender as a coffin nail.

The Modess sanitary napkin offered its revolutionary "silent purchase plan" to women suffering through the guilt years of the 1950s.

The plan turned out to be a coupon a woman could cut out of the magazine and hand to the pharmacy clerk so she wouldn't be embarrassed by having to ask for Modess out loud.

Dumb advertising existed even before there were dumb ad agencies.

Soldiers in the nineteenth century needed strong teeth to rip open rifle cartridges. Enterprising dentists harvested teeth from the strong young dead at the Battle of Waterloo and turned them into strong dentures, which they promoted as "Waterloo teeth."

A real estate ad in the hot housing market of Phoenix, Arizona, featured a photo of a woman realtor, who was slightly over the hill, posing with her pet poodle below the headline, "Top dog again this year." And smiling about it.

Dumb ads don't have to be created by professional ad agencies. Amateurs working newspaper classifieds can come up with doozies like these:

"Snowblower for sale. Only used on snowy days."

"Do something special for your Valentine: Have your septic tank pumped."

"Two wire-mesh butchering gloves: one 5-finger, one 3-finger."

A New York ad agency that represented several toy companies devised a new business pitch by sending stuffed toys and ransom notes to the executives of companies they were hoping to sign up.

In true kidnapping fashion, the notes were composed of words cut out of newspapers. The notes read: "We're holding your kid for ransom. We have their favorite stuffed animals. The kidnappers."

A cautious corporate executive passed one of the notes on to the FBI. Investigators determined that the note wasn't actually an extortion threat, just another ill-conceived idea by an adman who wasn't going to win a new account.

A California ad agency decided to treat potential clients to doughnuts, representing all the goodies the agency promised businesses if they signed up.

The agency demonstrated their sharp business sensibilities by sending the doughnuts through the mail. By the time prospective clients received the pitches and opened the boxes, they were treated to smashed doughnuts covered with mold, one of the few examples of truth in advertising.

Paris turned to an ad agency to convince dog owners to clean up after their pets. One ad shows a blind man with his white cane covered with dog excrement, as the announcer comments: "You're right not to clean it up. He does it very well for you."

Why are such ads necessary? Because Parisian dogs deposit ten tons of excrement on city sidewalks each day, and six hundred people end up in the hospital each year from slipping on it.

No wonder Paris is the City of Lights. Without the lights, no one would be safe walking there.

Designers for the wealthy are now promoting two-kitchen homes. One kitchen is for the family to gather for that old-time, around-the-stove, happy family meal.

What's the second kitchen for? That's where your cook does the actual cooking, as you wouldn't want her getting in your family's way.

In 1986 the ad agency for Gallo wines came up with a unique way to sell a new wine cooler. The agency created two fictitious farmers, naming the homey pitchmen Frank Bartles and Ed Jaymes (because James looked too ordinary).

Gallo ran a series of folksy TV ads with the two actors explaining that they had to take out a second mortgage on Ed's home to go into the wine business. The ads always concluded with Frank saying, "We thank you for your support."

When Frank announced in one commercial that he hoped people would buy more wine coolers because they needed the money, people actually wrote to the giant wine corporation, offering financial assistance to help cover the balloon payment on Ed's mortgage.

In 1883 a farm machinery manufacturer outraged veterans of the Civil War (and families of casualties) by promoting their reaper with a poster that depicted the Battle of Gettysburg interrupting a farmer at his harvest.

In 1954 a model demonstrated the dangers of live advertising on television when she was unable to open the door of a Westinghouse refrigerator to show off how easy it was to use.

Quaker Oats came up with a unique promotion in 1955: Buy some cereal, get a deed to land in the Yukon Territory—one square inch of it.

The cereal manufacturer bought 21 million of these miniplots from the Canadian government for $10,000. When the promotion didn't pan out, Canada took the land back for $37 in back taxes.

In 1964, when Pepsi's ad agency came up with the slogan "Come alive, you're in the Pepsi Generation," they didn't hire the best translators for international sales.

In German, the slogan became "Come alive out of the grave." In Chinese it was worse: "Pepsi brings your ancestors back from the dead."

The Marlboro Man, who rode tall in the saddle as he smoked his way through Marlboro Country, started out as the Marlboro woman.

Marlboros were originally marketed in the 1950s as a woman's cigarette, "mild as May," according to their less-than-successful ad slogan. The soon-to-be tough guy's cigarette even came with a red filter so the woman's lipstick wouldn't show up on the butt.

When that ad campaign flopped, Philip Morris simply switched horses in midstream and created a symbol of manhood out of a failed symbol of womanhood.

In the United States, opinion pollsters conduct 20 million interviews a year to find out what we want in our products—from cars to soda to political candidates. After all that research, they still don't know what we want—and neither do we.

Not content to put ads on the outside of buses, the inside of toilet stalls, projected onto the sides of buildings, video-displayed on gas pumps, and printed on the linings of airplane dinner trays—now they're sticking milk ads on the outside of bananas. When you prepare your morning cereal, the ads will remind you that if you've only got cereal and bananas in the bowl, then something's missing.

A Georgia high-school boy was suspended for wearing a Pepsi shirt on the school's Coca-Cola-sponsored "Coke in Education Day," during which students were requested to line up on the field for a photo and, in marching-band formation, spell out the word *COKE*.

Before W. C. Fields became a famous comic actor on stage and in movies, he worked as a juggler/drowner on a tourist pier in Atlantic City. When business was slow, he stopped juggling and waded into the ocean, where he pretended to drown.

The idea was that Fields's dramatic rescue by lifeguards would attract a crowd, so pier barkers could sell refreshments and Fields could go back to juggling. When business was slow, he drowned four times a day.

The pervasive influence of advertising allows for the transformation of anything into a sales tool. One man's art becomes an adman's pitch.

Consider this observation from writer William Burroughs about the free spirit who named the Beat Generation and the way marketers took advantage of the Beat vision of personal freedom: "[Jack] Kerouac opened a million coffee bars and sold a million pair of Levi's to both sexes."

The Ford Motor Company missed a chance at greatness when they turned down an endorsement offer, which came in the following letter: "While I still got breath in my lungs, I will tell you what a dandy car you make. I have drove Fords exclusively when I could get away with one."

The letter and the promotion offer came from Clyde Barrow, of the notorious, Hollywood-lionized bank robbers, Bonnie and Clyde.

Ford passed up another chance at uniqueness when the company was having trouble naming their new car in 1958. Executives got so desperate that they hired the poet Marianne Moore to come up with poetic names for the car.

She suggested several: Utopian Turtletop, Andante con Moto, Pastelogram, Intelligent Bullet, and Bullet Cloisonne.

Instead, Ford went with the Edsel, and the rest is history.

Famed adman Jerry Della Femina was in a brainstorming session, trying to devise a campaign slogan for his agency's electronics account, the Japanese manufacturer Panasonic.

Della Femina suggested the following headline for their ad: "From those wonderful folks who gave you Pearl Harbor."

It didn't fly, but Della Femina did make the gag work—as the title for his book about advertising.

In some businesses the surest way to lose business is to offer your merchandise at a reasonable price.

Helena Rubenstein, who made a fortune selling her own brand of expensive makeup, understood that you can't sell cosmetics to women unless you overprice it. "Some women won't buy anything unless they can pay a lot," she explained.

📖

Our final thought on the foolishness of advertising comes not from a businessman but from Arctic explorer Vilhjalmur Stfansson, who was not easily dazzled by bright lights.

"Unethical advertising uses falsehoods to deceive the public," he pointed out. "Ethical advertising uses truth to deceive the public."

Chapter 20

Dumb Crime

We never learn much about the clever criminals who get away with their crimes because they're smart enough not to tell us how they fought the law and won.

Then there are the dumb crooks:

A Detroit burglar took his dog with him on a 1968 break-in. When the cops showed up unexpectedly, the burglar ran off, leaving his dog behind.

The police caught up to the crook through a simple act of detection: They said to the dog, "Home, boy."

Police busted a San Antonio woman for possession of pot after an auto mechanic found eighteen packages of marijuana stashed inside the engine compartment of her car.

How did the mechanic stumble upon the grass? The woman had brought the car in for an oil change and didn't know that the mechanic would raise the hood to change the oil.

When a construction worker robbed a Fort Smith, Arkansas, convenience store, he didn't get caught because he was using a toy gun. The police caught him because he wore his hard hat during the robbery with his name written across the front.

☞

A Tampa, Florida, man handed a bank teller a note demanding cash. The police had no trouble catching up to the bank robber because he wrote the stickup note on his own pay stub, right below where his name and address were printed.

☞

The robber holding up a restaurant in Newport, Rhode Island, in 1975 was nervous and unpracticed at stickups. To stuff the money into his pocket, he used his gun hand. The gun went off, and he killed himself.

☞

A Texas man who killed his mother-in-law offered this novel defense: He thought she was a large raccoon.

☞

In Salinas, California, a woman was convicted of stealing credit cards to feed her addiction to Beanie Babies. "It was like a drug," she claimed. "Once I started, I couldn't stop."

How did she get started on a life of crime? Working at McDonald's, where her job exposed her to the larceny-inducing risk of stuffing the give-away toys into Happy Meals for kids.

A gang of eleven professional thieves pulled off one of the most successful robberies in history when they held up Brink's Boston headquarters in 1950, taking more than $2 million from the vaults, although they left behind another $800,000 in cash by mistake.

The crime went unsolved for years. Then eleven days before the statute of limitations was to expire, one member of the gang spilled everything to the police. Why? He felt cheated on his cut.

Thus, the perfect crime was thwarted by petty stupidity, a method of detection that has brought down more criminals than the superior intellects of any real-world Sherlock Holmes.

A defendant in a 1986 Illinois murder trial attacked his attorney in court, then punched the judge. After his conviction for murder, he appealed on the grounds that the attack had prejudiced the judge against him.

In 1978 a computer whiz manipulated a software program to steal $10 million by electronically transferring the money from a Los Angeles bank to his own bank account in Switzerland.

The only reason he got caught: He told someone what he'd done.

While on bail for the original crime, the electronic thief made a second illegal transfer, this time stealing $50 million. Authorities were watching him. He was sent to prison for both crimes.

In New York City each year nearly three times as many people are bitten by other people than are bitten by rats. These attacks prove not only that people are more dangerous than rats, but that rats have better taste.

∞

Right up there with the bungling burglars of the world are people who think they are safe-guarding their houses by installing burglar alarms.

The top six reasons burglar alarms are set off:

1. Homeowners trip the alarms by mistake.

2–5. The alarms are set off by temperature changes, forgotten windows left open, pets, and insects.

6. They're set off by party decorations such as helium balloons.

After all of those false alarms, burglars come in seventh.

Maybe after police solve the helium-balloon problem, they'll be able to do something about the burglary problem.

∞

In Virginia in 1998 a woman called the town jail and told officers that the prosecutor had dropped the charges on a man being held, so he should be released.

When officers explained they'd need that order in writing, the woman faxed a handwritten note alleging to be from the prosecutor. The note contained several misspellings and grammatical errors and was sent on a hand-drawn letterhead.

The police tracked down the sender through the fax number and arrested the girlfriend of the guy already in jail.

Singer Bobby Brown, Whitney Houston's husband, was allegedly drunk when he went into court to surrender so he could serve time for drunk driving.

Dumb crooks don't stop being dumb just because they're put in prison. That's where dumb crooks become dumb jailhouse lawyers, lawsuit-happy inmates with too much time on their hands.

These frivolous lawsuits came from New York convicts in 1998:

A burglar sued for $35,000 because he was served stale Pop-Tarts for prison breakfast.

An inmate alleged cruel and unusual punishment when he was denied deodorant while in solitary confinement.

🔗

A jury in the Los Angeles Superior Courthouse got into a fight during a break while they were watching Jerry Springer's guests fight on TV.

🔗

Playing with handcuffs, an Arizona man locked himself up, then couldn't find the key. Instead of calling a locksmith, he called the police to set him free.

While the cops were getting him loose from the hand-cuffs, they made a routine computer check, then arrested him on an outstanding warrant.

∞

A bank robber was busted after passing a Florida bank teller a stickup note written on the back of his parole card.

∞

Shooting for thief of the year award was the man who broke into a car, found a camera inside, and posed for pictures, which his girlfriend took, of him brandishing the screwdriver he used to break into the car.

It was a cheap camera, so the thief left it in the car. When the car was returned to its owner, he developed the pictures and found the ones of the car thief, who then posed for one more picture: a police mug shot.

∞

Two young men were charged with second-degree murder, attempted murder, and armed robbery of a Florida jewelry store. The men reportedly planned the job to raise money to pay their tuition at the Palm Beach Community College Police Academy.

∞

In Peoria, Arizona, Mom and Dad didn't want to drink and drive after a two-day binge. So they handed the car keys to their daughter and told her to drive them home.

Their daughter was eleven years old at the time. She crashed the car into a house. Her mother broke an ankle and some ribs in the crack-up, and both parents were charged with child abuse.

∞

A woman forger was arrested in Phoenix in 1998 for passing checks she'd stolen along with the victim's purse. She got caught when she misspelled the name on the checks she passed. Not only that, she misspelled it twice, wrong in two different ways, while she had the name right in front of her.

Also, the forger was in her twenties and handed over the victim's ID to cash the check. The victim pictured on the ID was twenty years older.

∞

In Florida a burglar was caught and convicted based on fingerprint evidence left at the scenes of the crimes.

The burglar was surprised because he'd been careful to wear gloves during each theft—golf gloves, the kind without fingertips.

∞

In Tukwila, Washington, a grab-and-run thief hustled out of a Target store with a stolen VCR. When employees followed him outside, they found that the thief couldn't start his van because he was out of gas.

The thief carried the VCR over to a gas station to buy gas. When police arrived, he was still filling up his van, with the stolen VCR under one arm.

An Ohio woman was sentenced to jail for two months over magazine subscriptions. The woman's crime? She got mad at three people in her town and forged their names to magazine subscriptions: 350 times.

〜

A Wisconsin man was arrested for firing a weapon illegally when he dragged his washing machine down the stairs and shot it three times with his pistol.

An original counterfeiter was arrested in Wichita, Kansas, for trying to pass two $16 bills at a hotel.

An Alabama Girl Scout leader was busted for stealing $700 in cookie money in 1982.

〜

In 1981 New York City's creative thieves came up with a new specialty: subway-token sucking. These thieves, who may have flunked pickpocketing, would place their mouths around subway turnstiles and suck the tokens back up out of the slots.

Police estimated that a competent token sucker could make about $75 a day.

A navy veteran was convicted of first-degree murder for killing his wife, who had filed for divorce. In his novel defense, the man admitted that he stabbed her multiple times, but said he didn't kill her because she was already dead.

The husband claimed he stabbed his dead wife to prevent their son from finding out she had committed suicide.

⊙ぬ

An off-duty Baltimore police officer, who worked in the antidrug unit, was out shopping for a car. On a test drive, he was surprised when the car salesman asked him to stop at one of the city's outdoor drug markets. He was even more surprised as he watched the salesman buy drugs from a known dealer.

When they returned the car to the dealership, the cop arrested the salesman, describing the arrest as "the most bizarre bust I've ever heard of."

⊙ぬ

The famed English barrister F. E. Smith trapped a con man who sued over an alleged arm injury during a bus accident.

The plaintiff painfully demonstrated that he could raise his injured arm only to shoulder level. Smith asked him how high he could lift his arm before the accident. The man demonstrated by raising his arm over his head, winning Smith's case for him.

⊙ぬ

Sadamichi Hirasawa convinced the clerks of a Tokyo bank to take some medicine, telling them that he was the bank doctor. The medicine was cyanide. As they died, he robbed the bank of $700.

When caught in 1948, Hirasawa got a life sentence instead of execution because lawyers convinced the judge that since Hirasawa knew he would be executed, the bank robbery was actually his way of committing suicide.

Japanese officials couldn't execute him, since their constitution prohibited suicide. Hirasawa was released from prison in 1980.

∽

One final thought on crime: It costs so much to keep thieves in prison that if we gave them the money we spent to house them, they wouldn't have any reason to steal.

Chapter 21

Avoidable Catastrophes

Planes are risky. Ships sink. Accidents happen—too often to too many people who had nothing to do with the cause but everything to do with the effect.

Then there are the avoidable accidents that happen because the people who were supposed to be in charge were asleep at the wheel of their brains.

The history of plane crashes usually involves a strange set of circumstances: bad weather, unexpected events, equipment problems. Same story for trains, ships, and industrial disasters.

But the pattern of unfortunate circumstances changes when augmented by mind melt. Then we suddenly become the bugs on their windshield.

The burning and sinking of the excursion steamship *General Slocum* in 1904 was caused by idiocy compounded by stupidity, resulting in the death of 1,031 people in New York's East River, most of them children on board for a Sunday school picnic.

The ship was seriously overloaded because of company greed. The bosses wanted the ticket money.

A fire started in a locked room in which flammable materials were stored in violation of safety regulations and common sense.

The fire hose didn't work because it had been sealed to prevent water leaks. When the seal was knocked loose, the hose burst under the water pressure because it hadn't been replaced or inspected in years.

The lifeboats were so tightly lashed to the decks that they could not be loosened. Some of the ship's life jackets had been nailed to the walls so customers wouldn't steal them.

Many of the life jackets wouldn't have done much good anyway, since they were stuffed with sawdust instead of cork. Some of these life preservers had been fitted with cast-iron bars so that instead of keeping the children afloat, they pulled them to the bottom of the East River.

The captain of a Portuguese sailing ship, the *St. James*, killed 450 passengers when he rammed the ship directly into a reef off the Cape of Good Hope in the late nineteenth century.

The captain never should have been anywhere near that reef. He had the ship running before a strong wind—at midnight, when he couldn't see the reef that the crew kept telling him was directly ahead of them.

The captain compounded his stupidity by deserting his foundering ship and its passengers in the one good lifeboat.

When the captain returned safely to Portugal, he was given another ship—which he rammed into another reef. This time he went down with the ship. If he hadn't, the officials in charge of astoundingly bad decisions would certainly have given him a third.

The owners of a grand new Chicago theater, the Iroquois, advertised in 1903 that it was fireproof. The city inspector agreed with them. However, the editor of a fire-prevention magazine warned them that the theater was a firetrap. He was ignored.

On December 30, a fire started onstage at the Iroquois and spread into the auditorium. People sitting in the orchestra section rushed out the fire doors to discover in midstep that the street was four feet below them. The first rush resulted in many broken bones, but these unfortunates served to break the falls of the people who came after them.

The balcony was the scene of the real tragedy. There were no exit signs. Most of the exit doors were locked and secured with iron grates. The doors that could be forced open led to fire escapes that had no ladders.

The fifteen-minute firestorm inside the theater killed 591 people, all of whom could have survived what started as a small stage fire if any sensible precautions had been taken.

Workers in a Russian collective in 1929 decided to celebrate the anniversary of the abdication of Czar Nicholas by getting drunk and watching a movie.

They had no theater, but commandeered a small factory room, although the factory manager told them it was too dangerous to pack so many people into a room where gasoline had been spilled on the floor.

They ignored him. The film was accompanied by a drunken accordion player, who tossed a cigarette onto the flammable film stock that piled up on the floor because the substitute projectionist didn't know how to run a projector.

The nitrate film ignited, which in turn set the gasoline-soaked floor ablaze in an overcrowded room, and 120 people died.

As for the factory manager who had tried to warn everyone off, he was beaten and killed by the survivors.

In a French disco called the Cinq-Sept Club, one of the main doors was locked once the crowd was inside. The other door was always sealed shut. One unlit fire exit was hidden behind the bandstand. The other exit door was blocked by stacked chairs. The club had neither fire extinguishers nor a telephone.

When a fire started in the club, all these dumb mistakes fed the blaze that killed 146 disco dancers in 1970.

Many of the early dirigibles crashed, but the most brainless crash can be pinned on politicians who ordered the Shenandoah to fly over a series of midwestern towns in 1925.

The ship's captain warned against taking off because of bad weather conditions. But local politicians convinced the Secretary of the Navy to order the dirigible into the air, against the captain's advice, so they could impress voters.

The Shenandoah crashed, killing fourteen crew members.

In 1957 the pilot of a chartered airplane crashed it, killing seventy-seven people aboard. Amazingly, the pilot had previously been fired by another airline for intentionally flying a plane into the ground—an incident that miraculously resulted in no deaths.

Under psychiatric care, the pilot had been declared unfit to fly. Although his record was known, the second airline hired him anyway.

In 1987 a ferry collided with an oil tanker in the Philippine Sea. Some three thousand people were killed in the explosion or drowned.

How did the ferry captain miss seeing the tanker in open water? He had given the bridge to an unqualified seaman because he wanted to take a break to watch a videotape and drink a beer.

Chapter 22

Intelligent Thoughts About Stupidity

Amazing how smart people are when they're talking about how smart people aren't.

The Persian poet Saadi outlined the paradox of intelligence: "A stupid person should keep silent. But if he knew this, he would not be a stupid person."

President Woodrow Wilson countered with this practical advice: "If a man is a fool, the best thing to do is to encourage him to advertise the fact by speaking. It cannot be so easily discovered if you allow him to remain silent and look wise. But if you let him speak, the secret is out."

Cowboy wisdom: "Never miss a good chance to shut up."

The twentieth century's most celebrated genius, Albert Einstein, noted: "Only two things are infinite, the universe and human stupidity, and I'm not sure about the former."

Author Elbert Hubbard agreed: "Genius may have its limitations, but stupidity is not thus handicapped."

Biologist Luther Burbank put man's wars, and the probable victor, in perspective: "Men should stop fighting among themselves and start fighting insects."

Transcendentalist Henry Thoreau observed man's ability to learn and grow: "Every generation laughs at the old fashions but religiously follows the new."

Feminist writer Erica Jong interpreted the relationships between men and women: "You see an awful lot of smart guys with dumb women, but you hardly ever see a smart woman with a dumb guy."

Austria's absurdist author Franz Kafka evaluated man's chances to improve his plight: "In a fight between you and the world, bet on the world."

Psychologist Carl Jung reflected upon his life's work: "Show me a sane person and I'll cure him for you."

Psychologist Havelock Ellis ranked his hope for man's improvement: "The place where optimism flourishes most is the lunatic asylum."

Social observer and humorist Will Rogers offered a solution to the Great Depression: "Stupidity got us into this mess. Why can't it get us out?"

Rogers also pointed out the undeniable: "Everybody is ignorant, only on different subjects."

British bicycle designer Mike Burrows, on a tour of America, came to an understanding of the American class system: "Marin County [California] was wonderful. The community was idyllic and the people were just beautiful. The whole town had nothing but beautiful people. I think there must have been an ordinance banning stupid and ugly people within city limits. Then I came to Las Vegas and realized what they had done with them all."

German philosopher Immanuel Kant grasped the difficulties of shaping man's fate: "From such crooked wood as that which man is made, nothing straight can be fashioned."

Attorney Clarence Darrow put the issues of his time into perspective: "History repeats itself. That's one of the things that's wrong with history."

Isaac Newton, one of the greatest scientific minds mankind has ever produced, didn't think much of mankind's achievements: "I do not know what I seem to the world, but to myself I appear to have been like a boy playing upon the seashore and diverting myself by now and then finding a smoother pebble or prettier shell than ordinary, while the great ocean of truth lay before me all undiscovered."

Sigmund Freud, father of psychoanalysis, probed the human mind until he came to this conclusion: "I have found little that is good about human beings. In my experience most of them are trash."

Upon further reflection, he added: "In the depths of my heart I can't help being convinced that my dear fellow men, with a few exceptions, are worthless."

Italian dictator Benito Mussolini also wasn't impressed by the good deeds of others: "The history of saints is mainly the history of insane people."

Writer Mark Twain faced up to our no-escape clause: "April 1, this is the day upon which we are reminded of what we are on the other 364."

Twain also observed: "It is better to keep your mouth shut and appear stupid than to open it and remove all doubts."

Acerbic author H. L. Mencken matched Twain's insight: "A man may be a fool and not know it. But not if he is married."

Humorist Dave Barry worked on newspapers long enough to realize: "If editors were so damned smart, they would know how to dress."

The life of the aristocracy has its pitfalls, as the duke of Gloucester pointed out: "The absurd thing about being a duke or a prince is that you are a professional ignoramus."

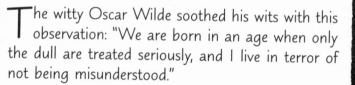

The witty Oscar Wilde soothed his wits with this observation: "We are born in an age when only the dull are treated seriously, and I live in terror of not being misunderstood."

Writer Edith Sitwell put a blunt edge to similar feelings: "I am patient with stupidity, but not with those who are proud of it."

Novelist Alexandre Dumas chose sides with a clear mind: "I prefer the wicked rather than the foolish. The wicked sometimes rest."

Henry IV, a sixteenth-century king of France, was listening to a pompous dignitary make a dull speech when a donkey started to bray. The king turned to the donkey and said: "Gentlemen, one at a time, please."

Scientist Arthur C. Clarke was smart enough to take a pragmatic approach to the workings of his own mind: "It has yet to be proven that intelligence has any survival value."

Medical researcher Oliver Sacks put life in perspective: "Nature gropes and blunders and performs the cruelest acts. There is no steady advance upward. There is no design."

College professor Frank Easterbrook countered a prevailing homily with this thought: "Some men achieve insignificance. Others have insignificance thrust upon them."

Star running back Knute Rockne took a common-sense view of his game: "The only qualifications for a [football] lineman are to be big and dumb. To be a back, you only have to be dumb."

Baseball pitcher Jim Bouton defended his sport: "Ballplayers often say, 'Quit thinking, you're hurting the club.' I really believe you can think too much in this game."

Playwright George Chapman found this truth for the ages in the sixteenth century: "Young men think old men are fools. But old men know young men are fools."

🔆

Writer Don Marquis outlined the dangers of intelligence: "If you make people think they're thinking, they'll love you. But if you really make them think, they'll hate you."

🔆

High-tech entrepreneur Guy Kawasaki contrasted smart craft with smart advertising: "Many expensive products are not indulgent—they are simply stupid—while some very inexpensive products are surprisingly indulgent. For example . . . a $20 haircut in Tokyo involves five attendants, a full upper-body massage, shaved eyebrows, four heated shampoos, and a parting gift."

🔆

Boston University president Daniel Marsh made this prediction in 1950: "If the television craze continues with the present level of programs, we are destined to have a nation of morons."

🔆

Biologist Stephen Jay Gould illuminated another side of intelligence: "Really bright people tend to be very modest in some overall cosmic sense, because they know how intensely ignorant we are about everything."

In 1776 economist Adam Smith saw clearly the effects of the industrial revolution on the human soul: "The man whose life is spent in performing a few simple operations of which the effects too are, perhaps, always the same or very nearly the same has no occasion to exert his understanding, or to exercise his invention. He generally becomes as stupid and ignorant as it is possible for a human creature to become."

In *Fiddler on the Roof*, the wise but poor Tevye observes: "If you're rich enough, no one will call you stupid."

The final word, but only for now, comes from an anonymous poem written in 1929 that makes the case for the equivocal nature of self-awareness: "See the happy moron. He doesn't give a damn. I wish I were a moron—my God, perhaps I am."

PART 2

Everything You Always Wanted to Know About Stupidity but Were Too Smart to Ask

Everything You Always Wanted to Know About Stupidity but Were Too Smart to Ask

Exactly how stupid are we?

We'll never know because we're exactly too stupid to figure it out. Unfortunately, we're just intelligent enough never to stop wondering about it.

Isn't intelligence the culminating achievement of nature?

If it were an achievement. But accidents don't count to our credit.

Nature has no long-range goals, no mission statements, no preference policies. Intelligence, the ability to fly, or a talent for chewing your way through dirt, it's all the same to nature—the coordination of millions of unrelated events running wild on an overoxygenated planet.

"There are six thousand species of mammals, none of which—outside the order of primates—is threatening to become a powerfully conscious species," biologist Stephen Jay Gould points out in the annoying manner of someone who knows what he's talking about.

"If intelligence was meant to be, you'd think it would have evolved convergently in lots of other lineages. It's just a weird invention that developed in one odd species living on the African savannas a couple of million years ago."

213

Who's dumber: primitive people or us?

Primitive people solved their problems. The solutions to the problems of civilized people only create more complex problems. We're short-term thinkers in a world of long-term consequences.

Primitive people were short-term thinkers too. But they lived in a short-term world.

Find food and survive pretty much encompassed the mental requirements of the ancient nomads, before they became attendants to the seed.

When these hunters, and their sidekicks the gatherers, came upon a hill, they went around it. They moved on with their lives.

We see a hill: We clear-cut it, strip-mine it, zone it, build a shopping mall on it. Later we moan about deforestation, soil erosion, air pollution, lousy shopping.

Then we try to move on through the twelve-step process of recovering hilloholics.

When primitive people got cold, they built a fire. We build atomic power plants.

Despite evidence to the contrary, we think we're more intelligent than our primitive ancestors. Still, the odds remain high that civilization's only lasting achievement will be the destruction of civilization.

Won't technology save us?

Science, the style of thinking practiced by people who are good at passing tests, is a complex machine for the production of poisons that nature could not produce in sufficient quantities herself.

Science examines our efforts to destroy the air, water, land, and everything that moves upon it, and devises clever ways to measure how we're doing.

Smart people might say: We're poisoning ourselves. Let's stop.

Scientists say: We're poisoning ourselves 4.78 percent less this year than we were doing last year. Let's issue a press release.

Is intelligence an independent attribute, or does it depend on what school you went to?

In 1982 two psychologists had a little fun, which in itself is news. They retyped, word for word, articles written by psychologists from Harvard, Princeton, and other top universities.

Well, they probably had their secretaries retype the articles. Or their grad students.

They changed the authors' names and institutions to colleges of less prestige, then resubmitted the articles to the same journals that had already published them.

Eight of the twelve articles were rejected as being not up to publication standards.

What would it be like if we were all smart?

Finland.

Every Sunday, we'd watch the National Curling League. Taco Bell would sell instant muesli. We'd have traffic jams on the bike paths to work each morning. Rival gangs of teenagers would hang out on street corners offering contrasting views on Hegelian philosophy in monotonal exhortations of blank verse.

Why are we so stupid?

We have to be. Nature designed us this way, the same way she designed gazelles to be quick and tigers to be terrifying.

If people weren't stupid, there goes cigarettes and triple bacon cheeseburgers, not to mention designer water and Brooklyn.

Civilization depends on masses of people making decisions that smart individuals thinking for themselves would never make.

Without dumb habits, we would all be living with the Amish, and the world would be run by people with sensible shoes. We'd go see big summer movies like *Nonlethal Tool*, *Live Easily*, and *Titanic Lessons in Proper Boat Safety*.

Are smart people dumber than stupid people?

The Chernobyl disaster in 1986, in which a Ukrainian nuclear reactor attempted to turn Europe into the ultimate New Jersey, was not a dumb error committed by dumb people.

It was a dumb error committed by smart people.

Operators ignored safety regulations under the theory that the reactor wouldn't explode because it hadn't exploded before.

Chernobyl's technicians frequently violated safety rules because they knew the rules had some built-in flexibility. Without this systematic stretch, the reactors would explode the second someone crossed the safety line.

So they played with the leeway and lost.

Dumb operators would have stuck with the rules. They wouldn't have been smart enough to think that the rules could cut them some slack.

Ask any army officer if he'd rather fight a battle with a squad of dumb soldiers or smart ones.

Smart soldiers will question orders because they know how often the orders are stupid and who's going to pay for bad decisions. Those confrontations are fine for movie dramatics, but a great way to get your squad shot to pieces in an actual firefight.

Dumb soldiers will follow orders to their death because they think they have to.

In the Civil War battle of Fredericksburg, wave after wave of Union soldiers charged across an open field and were mowed down by Confederates firing in safety from behind stone walls.

Some twelve thousand Union soldiers fell in those charges before the Rebel line was breached. You'd never find twelve thousand smart soldiers to follow those orders.

Scientists set up systems, like atomic reactors, that are far more intricate and unclear than operators can handle. We are clever enough to devise technology we're not intelligent enough to use.

We think we're as smart as our systems. We're not. Chernobyl wasn't an accident. It was an inevitability.

At least we learned our lesson from Chernobyl: Be careful; work smarter from now on.

Yeah, right.

Take the chain reaction set off by mistake in a Japanese nuclear fuel plant in 1999. Human error again. Fuel workers mishandled the enriched uranium they were processing and set off a chain reaction, resulting in radiation leakage that could have been disastrous.

Company execs blamed the uranium handlers, labeling them blunderers who took shortcuts so they could get off work early.

But these were veteran uranium workers, trained, aware of proper safety procedures. Why did they take shortcuts?

Because they could, same as Chernobyl.

Investigators accused company execs of encouraging workers to ignore correct procedures in order to speed up production.

It was Japan's sixth nuclear-handling accident in three years.

Is there any way our foreign policy could be more idiotic?

Apparently not, or our politicians would be voting it into effect right now.

American national policy since World War II has been based

on the School-Yard Bully theory of diplomacy: If you know we can beat you up, you won't force us to do it.

This approach might work if other countries weren't run by leaders as dumb as ours, people who base their national policies on the Oh Yeah? theory of government. When they meet up with a school-yard bully, they figure they'd better test him out to see if he's as tough as he says he is.

Our military and CIA carry out our bully policy around the world through a simple strategy: If we kill you now, we won't have to kill you later.

Which is the smarter choice: draft beer or Genuine Draft Beer?

Seems like a question of taste rather than of intelligence. But nothing is simple in an age where your share of the advertising costs more than your share of the beer.

Real draft beer is better if you like good beer. Genuine Draft Beer is better if you want to marvel at how marketers can make millions by continually lowering the bottom of the barrel we live in.

Draft beer comes from a barrel. You hold the glass up to the tap, and the beer falls out. Makes for better beer, as any English pubster can explain, if you're buying.

Genuine Draft Beer comes in bottles or cans, the opposite of draft beer. They can legally call nondraft beer draft beer by the international law that states: If you can make big money out of a lie, go ahead.

First, the boss says: Let's go for quality—as long as it doesn't cost more, take more time, or drag me away from my golf game.

Then the marketing masters step in and make the beer better through the use of better words.

And sometimes pictures.

Particularly pictures of sexy young women, who if they actually drank the nondraft draft beer would turn into fat blowsy women, the kind men drink beer to forget.

Are hard workers dumber than bums?

Consider the bum: no money, no place to sleep, no food, no lovers, no season tickets, no prospects. Yet there must be something attractive about the proposition, or so many people wouldn't be entering the profession.

There is a lure: no work.

That's the only advantage a bum life has to offer—and it's enough.

As the rest of us rush off to work too fast every morning, fight the traffic, get steamed by coworkers who don't do their share and bosses who know less than the idiots who had the job before them; as we put in too much time making the owners rich, only to fight the traffic to get back home, only to do it all over again the next day—they don't.

Not working seems to balance out all the alleged benefits that work provides.

Has it always been the worker vs. the shirker? Let's trace the progress of the career man.

Prior to civilization, there were unlimited opportunities for all men, women, and children to work. The job was called survival.

The basic job skills: Find something to eat; keep warm; don't get hit on the head with a rock.

Sounds simple enough. But all jobs have drawbacks: bosses, saber-toothed tigers, cubicle psychology, the tendency of other people in your field to look for the same warmth or the same food to kill rather than share.

Still, compared to the job insecurities that comprise civilization, those were the good old days.

Because people followed where dinner led, companies remained small and competitive, clan-sized operations. There were no prehistoric corporations insisting that we wear the badger tie with the mammoth skin suit on the daily hunt.

Civilization brought with it the first curse of mankind: farming.

Farming was hard work and a slow way to produce dinner; although once it did, it also produced lunch and breakfast.

The working farmer was obligated to stay in one place, as anchored to the cubicle of his farm as we are to our desks.

Stationary dinners gave rise to the second curse of the working class: the nonworking class.

These people recognized early on that there was no point in everyone doing the same hard work if someone else was going to do the hard work anyway.

They became kings, priests, and thieves, the nonworking class.

Thieves led to defense. Defense led to offense. Offense led to armies. Armies led to bigger armies. Bigger armies led to generals. Generals led to corporations, and that's how we got into the mess we're in today.

That fantastic structure of nonwork rests on the back of the little turtle down at the bottom of the stack: the Yertle worker. The cannon fodder, mill fodder, PC fodder.

The worker always gives more than he gets to the company he works for. If he got more than he gave, he wouldn't be a worker. He'd be the boss.

Meanwhile, the bum contemplates our folly without worrying that he will be down-sized. He will not be replaced by someone half his age willing to be a bum for half the pickings.

The bum has the one thing workers can never have: job security.

But surely we're smarter than we used to be?

Regular people in the tenth century could muddle through their entire lives without meeting a smart person. They never felt dumb by comparison.

Perhaps they couldn't figure how to shut out the drafts in the winter or grow enough turnips to give themselves that well-fed feeling, but neither could anyone else they knew.

To them, the world was just a drafty place with insufficient turnips.

They knew no one who wore Gore-Tex while they shivered damply, or who dined at five-star restaurants while they ate at Turnip King.

Now we live in the green age of jealousy. We're envious of movie stars who have sexier lovers than we do, software kings who have more money, and politicians who get away with better lies than we would dare tell at the corner bar.

People who score 550 on their college entrance exams feel they're smart enough. They'll be going to the same school as the brains they made fun of in high school.

They don't get it. They're being let into college so they can finance the education of the smart kids. Colleges need their tuition money so they can give scholarships to the brains.

If they only let smart kids into college, America would be able to get by with a half dozen universities. The rest of the schools could open NFL franchises.

What do those 550 scorers learn in college? How to throw keggers without throwing up.

The lowest score anyone can get on an SAT is 200. Why not zero? Because the college board doesn't want people to think they have zero intelligence.

Who is smarter: your boss or you?

You are.

The boss has money, the power and perks, the authority to act like he knows what he's doing when he's actually wondering how long till people find him out. He's got membership in the rich guys' club, where they sit around trying to top one another with ways to torture employees in the name of human resource development.

But the bosses don't have the brains.

We can prove that in three ways:

1. During the boss's absence, any secretary in the world could fill in and do the job better. But no boss could do their secretary's work.

2. On the average, 60,000 Americans have the good sense to quit their lousy jobs every day. But bosses only have enough sense to fire 12,000 people a day. Bosses are too dumb to fire 48,000 people who hate their jobs and are getting ready to prove it.

3. If your boss was smarter than you, he'd make sure you liked him. Only stupid bosses create resentful employees.

But bosses don't care about being liked because they are the new royalty. The goal of this elite is not to make a better product, or a better world, or even a more profitable company. Their goal is to make the process so complex that only they can operate it.

It's like basketball. You may be the best player at the Y on Saturday morning, hitting a high percentage of your shots, playing smart D. When you see film from the NBA as the game was played forty years ago, you say to yourself, "Man, they were slow and clunky back then. I could play better than that."

Probably you could. But the game has been raised to such a

complexity of height, speed, and agility that you would be run off the court, even by the Los Angeles Clippers.

That's why those arrogant, loafing players make millions. They have successfully specialized the game to the point where only they can play it.

The elite are doing the same thing to us everywhere.

Eventually, we'll all be asking them, "You want fries with that?"

We've been stupid for so long, can we still find original ways to do something dumb?

Absolutely. We're doing it all the time.

In southern California, a man gazing through a telescope from his house overlooking the beach spotted a pink Corvette on the sand. The car was about to be swamped by waves from the incoming tide. Worried that someone might be incapacitated inside the car, he called the police.

The cops couldn't find a car on the beach—pink, Corvette, or otherwise.

When they went up the bluff to the man's house and looked through his telescope, they figured out what the man couldn't: He had the scope trained on a toy car a kid had left in the sand.

Who's dumber, men or women?

Only men are dumb enough to ask that question.

Women simply look at what men have achieved with their dominion over the world and know there's no way they could have messed it up as badly.

Still, if women are so much smarter than men, why haven't they taken over?

Perhaps the answer is hidden in this separation statistic: After divorce, 58 percent of the men say they're happier; but 85 percent of the women say they're happier.

Are religious people smarter than the nonreligious?

Most religions agree upon the worship of a supreme God who created the universe and demands of His people high moral standards of behavior.

In the name of this one God and our high moral standards, the devout of all religions have slaughtered one another for centuries.

Everyone calls for this spiral of slaughter to stop in the name of God.

It never stops.

Peace is a temporary cease-fire during which the various sides reload.

How can we account for this persistence in the endless slaughter of the children of God in the name of a loving God who demands the end of slaughter?

Comfortably, it turns out.

It's the difference between the true religion of the one God fighting against the evil heathens of the false god.

Ours is the former. Theirs is the latter.

It's true throughout history and from all sides toward the middle. We are all someone else's heretic.

Is there a one-religion race in another galaxy, where aliens know God and celebrate the universe in some way other than trying to destroy it?

Not if God made them like us.

Is the lottery the dumbest possible way to get rid of excess money?

No, we'll invent something dumber as soon as the Bright Boys get through with their research.

Meanwhile, lotteries combine two of our most popular mental weaknesses: gambling and advertising.

Does every state lure the gambling-positives with the same slogan logic: "You can't win if you don't play"?

As with most advertising, you'd be better off betting against the pitch. The only truth about the lottery is that you can't lose if you don't play.

Odds on winning big in the lottery are so bad you'd be better off taking all the money you have, putting it in a sock, giving that sock to the first stranger you meet on the street, and saying, "Here, if by some chance you make $10 million with this money, find me and give me $1 million, okay?"

You don't even have to be good at math to know you can't win the lottery. The state lottery is run by the government. When was the last time you beat the government at anything?

If you could make money through the lottery, then rich people would play and they don't. They fly off to Vegas, where they also don't make money, but at least are made to feel important. When was the last time the mini-mart made you feel important for blowing the milk money on a few lottery tickets?

Who's dumber, the judges or the attorneys?

We leave that tough call to Judge Thurman Arnold, who resigned from the U.S. court of appeals and returned to private practice, saying, "I'd rather have to talk to a bunch of damn fools than listen to them."

Is it a smart idea to take advice?

Here's the only advice you should ever take: Don't ever take advice.

Sounds like advice, but it's not advice. That's a paradox, and the whole point of a paradox is that you can't follow it.

Actually, there could be some advice worth taking. Unfortunately, it's not the kind people give out.

Nearly everyone who knows what they're doing keeps it to themselves. If they shared it, then everyone would know what they knew and it wouldn't work anymore.

Who's smarter: dumb beasts or dumb men?

President John Tyler buried his favorite horse with these words inscribed on the tombstone: "Here lies the body of my good horse, the General. For 20 years he bore me around the circuit of my practice and in all that time he never made a blunder. Would that his master could say the same!"

People frequently honor their laudable pets and other beasts of our burdens. No animal has left an epitaph for a man.

Is it smarter to try try again or quit while you're ahead?

When we say quit while you're ahead, we really mean quit while you're behind but not by too much.

In reality you're never ahead. All life is 6–5 against, as Damon Runyon once pointed out. That's why realists invented the moral victory and the close one, in hopes of slowing down the rate of failure.

However, if you try try again, you're more likely to sink deeper by finding new ways to lose than if you had quit when you weren't too far behind. There are always more ways to lose than to win.

There is one strategy that can bring victory: Encourage others to try try again, then observe their failures.

When it's your time to step up, you will know what to avoid and have a better chance to get ahead early, at which time you should offer your opponents a chance for a moral victory, so they will feel good about quitting while they're not too far behind.

When you leave defeated opponents happy, they are more likely to accept a close defeat next time.

Finding enough people who are satisfied with moral victories is how you get on a winning streak.

Who's dumber: a moron or an idiot?

The moron is the guy who speeds past you recklessly on the right, while the idiot is the guy in front of you going too slow, forcing you to pass him on the right.

Or is it the other way around?

We have become so accustomed to thinking of idiots and morons as everyone who gets in our way that we forget that they were once technical terms.

The idiot was an adult who had the brains of a three-year-old kid. The moron was doing much better; he had the brains of an eight-year-old.

Look around you. If you find enough morons with the brains of eight-year-olds, you're probably living in a college town.

What about Harvard and Stanford? Doesn't get much smarter than that, does it?

Or so they'd have us believe.

As an experiment, we sent the following letter to one hundred Harvard professors and one hundred Stanford professors:

"I'm writing a book about stupidity/intelligence and thought you might like to participate by answering the following question:

What's the stupidest thing you've done?

My theory is that really intelligent people are exceptional in their dumb moments also."

We got back the following responses:

Harvard: 2

Stanford: 1

From Harvard professor J. H. H. Weiler came this reply: "Answering this E-mail would be way up on the list."

From Stanford professor Tom Wasow:

"In 1982 I was invited to give a talk to the International Congress of Linguists in Tokyo. I also agreed to give several other talks at Japanese universities.

"The night before I was to leave, my wife asked if I needed a visa for Japan. I was certain I didn't.

"The next day, when I checked in at the airport, the clerk informed me that I couldn't board because I had no visa. She told me I had to get to the Japanese consulate in San Francisco that afternoon (it was Friday, and the consulate would be closed over the weekend) and convince them to give me an expedited visa.

"Since I would miss my flight, I would also have to go to the airline office and rebook. On reflection, I decided that the chances of being able to accomplish all this in one afternoon were so slim that I should give up on the whole trip.

"I walked out of the terminal in a daze and got on the bus. When the bus reached the freeway, it turned north (toward San Francisco), not south (toward my home in Palo Alto) as I had expected.

"Once in San Francisco, I figured I might as well see whether I could get the visa and the ticket changed. Much to my surprise, I was able to do so that afternoon, and I made it to Japan a day late.

"This incident could be taken as illustrating one thing about my life that has been extraordinary: my luck. Here I did two really stupid things (not getting a visa and taking the wrong bus), and they more or less canceled each other out!"

From Harvard professor Nikolaas J. van der Merwe:

"I grew up in South Africa and have done fieldwork on most continents. One colleague has described me as the best person to have in a nasty spot in a foreign place, but not everybody will agree. However, I am an instrument-rated pilot, have cruised the upper Amazon and Orinoco (and Okavango swamps) in dugout canoes, and know from experience which vehicles can cross Africa from north to south with a reasonable chance of success (hardbody Land Cruiser, Hi-lux 4WD, Land Rover 109).

"So here I am living in a house hidden in the trees near Concord, Massachusetts. My mailbox is a quarter mile away, and I have to drive across the neighbors' land to get there.

"One Sunday morning last winter, I put the coffee on, and went down the driveway to pick up the *New York Times*. This involved getting in my dressing gown, shoes untied, into the four-wheel-drive Mazda pickup.

"At the mailbox, I find the *Times* lying on the ground, so I turn the pickup around in the road and stop next to the paper, headed back up the driveway. I open the door and lean out to pick up the paper, *with my feet on the clutch and brake*.

"I fall out the door. The pickup, its engine on fast idle in the cold, takes off by itself. It takes down about fifty feet of my neighbors' fence, then heads across their lawn and ends up in their stream, its engine stalled.

"Meanwhile, I'm running after the vehicle, but the wet earth near the stream sucks my shoes off. Eventually, I find my shoes and get in the vehicle.

"At this point, the four-wheel-drive becomes properly useful for the first time in its life, and I pull out of there, pick up the paper, and go home.

"I had to explain the problem to the neighbors. That was okay; money fixed the damage. But my field-working colleagues were not nearly so accepting. *You had your feet where?*"

Apparently, 197 other learned professors at these top universities have never done anything stupid. Or hope we'll believe that.

Why are people who have careers invested in intelligence afraid to admit their foibles, follies, and failures? Do they worry that if we think they're human, it will devalue their brain stock, as the rich fret over money when they already have enough?

This experiment wasn't meant to embarrass the few professors who participated, or even those many who participated by not participating.

The confessions of the brave are intended to comfort the rest of us with the realization that intelligence and stupidity are not mutually exclusive but fully compatible.

If the brightest among us can pull dumb stunts, then the rest of us shouldn't be so quick to kick ourselves for our own screwups.

Instead, we should think about applying for teaching positions at Stanford and Harvard.

Is it smarter to tell people how you really feel, or to keep it to yourself?

When people say, "Tell me how you feel," what they really mean is, "Sit still while I tell you how I really feel."

Sharing your innermost thoughts is only smart if you're in a college psych class and are trying to turn it into a rap session so you can get a good grade without having to write another term paper.

Feelings are like body odors. Everyone has them, but we'd rather you covered yours up.

Whining, however, makes a lot of sense.

Moaning and groaning are strategies that fit almost every occasion. Unlike feelings, complaining has a definite upside: The more you whine about how terrible everything is, the longer God lets you live because He sees that you get it.

In the face of so much evidence to the contrary, why do we insist that we're smart?

We need to feel smart because it makes us feel safe, as if we will have the wits necessary to deal with life's daily dangers.

Despite childproof caps on our medicine and insurance agents with giant soft hands, we are not safe from a world with more dinks than caresses.

If we did not feel smart enough to cope with assistant managers, ozone depletion, and phone solicitors, civilization as we want to know it would crimble, which is what happens when something isn't even smart enough to crumble.

A sense of intelligence works as a security blanket. If we were smarter, we'd realize that there is no security, that civilization is like a bus shelter: It may keep you dry in the rain, but you can't stay there forever.

In fact, we're only intelligent enough to fool the only people we have to fool: ourselves.

We live in a complex world. Isn't complexity a sign of intelligence?

All the great religions and spiritual traditions of the world guide us down the path of simplicity. Many of them state quite clearly that you cannot know enlightenment until you rid yourself of all worldly obsessions. Yes, that includes your remote control.

Aren't you confusing wisdom with intelligence?
Only a society without wisdom would insist on its intelligence.

So it's smart to be wise?
Not if you work for a living.

Corporations prefer people who are good at pushing buttons and having their buttons pushed.

Businesses do not want their employees pursuing wisdom, unless the pursuit of wisdom is listed in the goals and practices section of their mission statement, probably subgoal 47.3 (see your supervisor for details).

Then there are companies that pursue wisdom?
There are companies that pursue wisdom consultants because they already have run through management consultants, time-utilization consultants, problem-solving consultants, and even consultant-coordinating consultants.

They turn to wisdom consultants if they have funds left over in their consultant budget, because they realize that if they turn the extra money back into the company's general fund, they will get less funding in next year's budget.

But don't these consultants teach wisdom?
You cannot teach wisdom. You can only learn it.

Any coach can tell you how to hit a baseball. But you will never get a hit until you step up to the plate and start swinging for yourself.

No one likes living in overcrowded cities, yet millions do it in the world's densest: Manila, Shanghai, Cairo, Paris, Bombay. Why aren't they smart enough to move?

They're waiting for everyone else to smarten up and move out. Then their cities won't be so unlivable.

Paris, ah, the City of Lights. It's such a beautiful city, surely we can jam another million people in there.

But won't that make it miserable for everyone?

Not if we keep telling them: Paris, ah, the City of Lights.

In this way we counter any smart move we make simply by making too many of them. There's nothing good we can't dumb down.

Overpopulation is not just a global problem. It's a marketing solution.

Was America founded by the brains or the jerks?

The first European who stumbled upon America thought he'd found India, so we didn't get off to a great start.

The next group of laterally mobile Europeans were called explorers because no one erects statues to looters, which is an Indian word for "here come those lost guys in their big ships to steal anything we haven't nailed down, and isn't it a shame we didn't invent nails before they got here?"

The natives—smart and stupid—had been living quietly in America (or Our Place, as they mistakenly called it back then), not needing nails to deal with one another.

They psychically floated back to Europe the notion that the earth was flat in hopes of keeping the Europeans from falling into their laps.

Didn't work. The quest for loot was simply too strong. The explorers were willing to risk falling off the end of the world because that was still better than being poor in Europe.

Looting is a sign of intelligence, recognizing that a system of governance isn't strong enough to stop looters, in which case the looters are going to become the new system of governance, so you might as well get what you can, or they're going to erect a statue to the next guy.

These early looters took their stolen wealth back to Europe because the natives had neglected to set up shopping malls in America.

Returning to Europe was not a sign of intelligence, as rent was higher and very few looters were able to keep their loot once they got back, where they found that even smarter looters were waiting for their return. But they had to go back to the Old World because at the time there was simply nothing to buy in the new one.

If there had been, the early explorers would have stayed, everyone in Europe would have assumed they'd fallen off the edge of the world, and Americans would now be eating at McGeronimo's and watching the NLF (National Lacrosse Federation) on the tube every Sunday instead of the NFL.

The next group to come to America were our four fathers: the British, the Spanish, the French, and the Miscellaneous.

These people were definitely brains because they devised a more efficient method of looting: Stay in the New World and steal its resources without giving the stay-at-home looters a share. The colonial spin doctors called this business theory the American Revolution.

The natives were too smart to do all the back-breaking work this kind of strip-mining and deforestation required because they'd been getting along just fine without doing it.

So the bosses had to import a labor pool, which they did by persecuting the poor of Europe, in an attempt to make their lives so miserable that they'd leave.

This plan had limited success. Turned out that many poor people were used to being miserable and preferred to be persecuted in their own hometowns, rather than drown on the way to America.

When the bosses couldn't get enough European poor to exploit the resources of America, they kidnapped a work force from Africa and gave them minimum-wage jobs in America, the minimum wage being a plate of bad food a day.

Now that slavery has been abolished, the minimum wage for lousy jobs is just enough money to buy a plate of bad food a day.

So the answer is, America was settled by brains and jerks and plenty of them.

What's the smart thing to do about crime?

There are thousands of armed robberies in the United States every year. This field of work is getting so crowded that armed robbers are often forced to rob one another.

In Iceland there has been only one armed robbery in the country's history.

We need to educate America's armed robbers so they grow smart enough to move to Iceland, where there's no competition.

Is it stupid to keep a gun in the house?

Depends. Were you also planning to keep bullets?

Three Americans are killed by guns in the house every day. That's three houses today where people now realize they would have been smarter to get rid of their guns.

On the other foot, one American a day dies in bathtub accidents. So we would be smart to get rid of baths too.

Is it smarter to marry for love or for money?

Some of America's native tribes had a smart system: Anyone rich and powerful was forbidden to marry anyone from another rich family. Instead, the rich had to marry someone from a poor family.

Using that system, there was no tribal CEO making one thousand times what everyone else made, and people at the bottom knew they weren't going to stay there forever.

These sensible tribes were wiped out by Europeans, who came to America preaching freedom, which they achieved by annihilating everyone else.

The Europeans had a system of marriage that has become the world standard: The rich and powerful can marry anyone they want. The poor and powerless can marry anyone the rich don't want.

Back to you.

If you marry for love, your condition can be cured. People who are in love eventually won't be.

Therefore, it's smarter to marry for money, as long as you remember the first rule of successful prostitutes: Get the money up front.

As surely as you marry for money, you will be traded in for the same reason. Being rich means never having to say: "Can I afford the new model, the one with the shinier gadgets?"

While marrying for money is smarter than marrying for love, it's not much smarter. If you marry for love, you're doomed to fall out of love. If you marry for money, you're doomed to be kicked out.

There must be a smarter system, and there is—because you can't get divorced unless you get married first.

Without marriage, you can fall in love as much as you want and not worry about whether this is the one person you should marry. There is no one you should marry, only someone you do marry.

If the person you're in love with insists on getting married, stall like crazy. Stalling is a strategy of intelligence, a prime way to solve problems. Eventually, you'll fall out of love, and the question will become moot.

As for money, if you're so smart, don't marry for it. Go out and get some of your own. Then you'll know what it's like to have someone want to marry you for your money.

Should you try to improve yourself? Or are self-help programs just a waste of time?

Everything is a waste of time.

Half a million Americans a year try cosmetic surgery to improve their looks.

Look around you. You won't see half a million better-looking people each year.

Can dumb people still enjoy life?

You have to be dumb to enjoy life. If you get too smart, you see the flaws in the plan.

Death, that's a big one, gets in the way of any kind of sustained fun.

Disease, injury, depression, oppression, repression, regression, obsession, and group sessions—all flaws in the plan of life, which when originally designed was: Run free; find pleasure.

You don't need intelligence for that.

Intelligence will always impede enjoyment because the brain would rather be analyzing: What is enjoyment? What is true enjoyment? How can I tell if I'm really enjoying myself, or only think I'm enjoying myself? What do I mean by enjoyment? What do I mean by life? What do I mean by what do I mean?

Meanwhile, that dumb jerk next door is riding his muscle car across someone's meadow with his arm around some bunny babe, and his brain is going right along with his arm.

Are people growing smarter or dumber?

Smart people are getting smarter, which causes the rest of us to get dumber by comparison. As the bar gets raised higher, we're turning into a nation of limbo brains.

Smart people used to swallow hemlock for the good of the idiots in society. They used to let morons burn them at the stake, failing to convince the fire-happy dummies that just because they could think it didn't make them heretics.

Then smart people wised up. They packed us into overcrowded cities so we would be more reluctant to start bonfires.

They convinced us to pay for their scholarships to Stanford and MIT, so they could make easy livings as engineers and lawyers.

They run the corporations that run the world. They are no longer heretics because they now control the computer program that controls the heretic-labeling apparatus.

How did the smart ones turn the tables on us, transforming themselves from the persecuted into the princes of the world?

They learned the art of pacification.

People who are not too bright are generally contented when left alone in an emotionally neutral muddle. The smart ones learned how to mass-produce muddle the way Henry Ford massproduced cheap cars.

In the Dark Ages, the world's princes pacified the none-toobright by slaughtering them. With the Enlightenment, the smart ones who couldn't manage slaughter effectively came up with better diversions: gadgets.

They pacify us with VCRs and SUVs, with Prozac and the Internet, with spectator sports and shopping malls.

Big Dumb Lunks used to take pleasure in crushing the necks of smart guys. Now BDLs take pleasure in using their remote controls to channel surf. TV turns a BDL's hovel into a realm, and the remote gives him control of that magic kingdom, the most controllable realm he'll ever get his hands on.

Hands busy massaging buttons won't be crushing scrawny necks.

Now and then Big Dumb Lunks rise up and need to hit something. So the smart ones have invented ways to neutralize their muscle by killing them from a distance, where strength and courage are no longer required.

Back in sword days, the world was ruled by stout shoulders and big biceps, while smart weaklings cowered in the corner calculating the varying degrees of unfairness in approaching death.

But the head brains got revenge by learning how to slaughter muscle heads by the thousands with the push of a button. They didn't actually need a button. Could have used a lever. But levers require a biceps.

As for evolution of the intelligence of Big Dumb Lunks, it's carefully monitored by the brains. Anytime they see the threat of a breakout, they release another gadget to pacify the restless.

We get compact disc players, mobile phones, Net-surfing computers—all issued with user guides that undermine the efforts of BDLs to rise up by proving to them that they'll never understand how anything works. They'll have to be satisfied to sit back and push the buttons.

As soon as the brains invent a button that gives instant orgasms, the BDLs will never rise up out of their La-Z-Boys again.

Who's smarter, Democrats or Republicans?

Democrats know the rich won't vote for them, except for confused movie stars. Republicans know the poor won't vote for them, except for one guy in Cleveland who hasn't figured it out yet.

So they both work the middle.

The Republicans try to convince the middle that unless they have Republicans in office, the Democrats will turn them into poor people; while the Democrats try to convince the middle that no one will turn them into rich people, ever.

Therefore, the only intelligent politicians—Democrat or Republican—are the ones who lose the election. Once they're out of office, they'll leave you alone, and that's about as intelligent a result as we can ask for.

Doesn't coping with a difficult world imply intelligence?

Cavemen didn't have day planners. Or lawyers.

You might think that makes us smarter—dealing with incredibly complex lives day after day.

But barbarians didn't have therapists either. No one thought of encouraging Attila the Hun to get in touch with his feelings. Attila and the Huns expressed themselves all too clearly.

Because we can operate computers and negotiate the labyrinth of self-improvement, we assume that takes superior brains.

You think it was easy to operate a horde of screaming Huns so you could conquer half the world?

We're still screaming like barbarians as we charge down the circuits of our control chips and master complex ways to simplify our lives so that we can feel good about ourselves from 2:40 to 3:05 every other Thursday.

Knowing which buttons to push doesn't make us smart. It just makes us better at pushing buttons.

What's the stupidest thing mankind has done to itself?

Invent guns and use them. Guns made killers out of losers.

Before guns, when you wanted to kill someone you had to get within counterstrike range, which required courage, skill, strength, and luck.

Guns changed the basic premise of killing from Thou shalt kill if thou can, to If you can reach them from farther away than they can reach you, then you can kill them before they kill you.

Now we have pilots who sit a mile up in the sky and kill thousands of people they never see, then go home and have dinner that was cooked in a factory ten thousand miles away, get up in the morning, and kill a few more thousand faceless people who will soon have no faces.

Human beings can see problems coming and figure out ways to solve a crisis before it strikes. Doesn't this unique predictive intelligence make us special?

In the same way that having long necks makes giraffes special. Everyone stares at us, but that doesn't mean we're going to beat the odds in the long run.

For all our abilities to analyze and prepare for disasters, we have equal talents for misanalyzing.

We take disaster-aversion maneuvers that shift us directly into the path of a worse disaster. We create new crises that never would have come about if we hadn't been trying to preempt the crisis we thought was coming.

The best analytical minds of the early 1900s assured us that if we banded together and defeated Germany in World War I, we would put an end to war.

This predictive, crisis-aversion strategy succeeded in creating an even more destructive war twenty-five years later.

When we read in the Bible that the meek shall inherit the earth, we, in our inexhaustible vanity, assume that we're the meek, even though the human race is the most arrogant killer the life force has ever devised.

The truly meek, who will inherit the earth by surviving us, cannot predict the future and have no need to. Look under your heel. They scurry in the dark and are surprisingly hard to stomp out.

If cockroaches could laugh, or had any reason to, they would be laughing at us.

But the human race has produced Plato, Shakespeare, Emerson. How can you say we're not smart?

Emerson? Didn't he play for the Red Sox? Good trivia question, man. How many points did we score?

Consider that 99.9 percent of the race that produced these great thinkers have never heard of them, read their writings, or thought about their ideas. Yet they manage to live their existences of brutish pain and brutish pleasure without having any reason to seek the advice of philosophically committed nonbrutes.

If the greatest minds the human race has produced serve any purpose, it's to distract teenagers with college. Without college, students would be forced into the cold world, where they'd suffer like their parents, who are too busy thinking that no matter how hard they work they can't keep up, to worry about whether they're heeding the timeless wisdom of Plato or the enlightened advice of Emerson.

Exactly how did Einstein make a living and does he have any good stock tips? If Plato had pondered the realities of the investment portfolio, then he would have been of some worth to his fellow human beings.

Are stupid people stupid? Or just differently intelligent?
While our society pays lip service to the notion of equality, lip service is generally as far as anyone in power cares to go. There is no promise of equality of brains.

However, stupid people are almost as smart as smart people, but that's only because smart people aren't as smart as they think they are.

Fortunately, stupid money is just as good as smart money. Politicians and marketers assume they can separate stupid people from their money easier than they can smart people, which is easy enough.

Plenty of political careers have been built around cornering the stupid vote and letting the brains fume over lost opportunities. Advertising is at its most effective when campaigns are pitched to the stupid psychographic segment of the buying public.

Remember that commercial about the guy so dumb he has to write his shopping list—he wants a soda—on the back of his hand because he gets so dazzled by the merchandise that he always forgets what he went into the mini-mart for?

Then, uh oh, he sticks his hand in the cold soda barrel and the ink washes off. Now he's stuck. But not to worry. He'll feel right at home in our store.

Are stupid people going to ruin it for the rest of us?
Not a chance. Smart people will.

Stupid people should take comfort in their moral superiority because nearly all of the really horrendous travesties throughout history were perpetrated by smart people.

It takes superior brainpower to build atomic bombs that can destroy everyone we're mad at, along with everyone we like and everyone we've never met, then decide that that's not enough, we need variety in our self-annihilative devices, so let's also design chemical and biological weapons that can do the same job, only leaving behind, when all the humans get radiated into the next plane of existence, less of a charred mess, because it's well known that cockroaches do not care to sweep up.

If dumb people wanted to destroy the human race, they'd grab a brick and go around hitting everyone over the head, which would take several centuries to get the job done.

Smart people can wrap it up in a couple of hours. Intelligence may turn out to be nothing but efficiency attached to motivation.

How can I tell if I'm stupid?

You can't.

If you are stupid, then you're too dumb to know it.

If you're smart, then you are no doubt smart enough to doubt yourself.

When your mother says, "What a smart boy you are," ask for a second opinion. She'd probably say the same thing if you were a blabbering idiot, which you may be for all you know, since it's impossible to know.

You certainly can't trust the experts. If they say you're stupid, they may be too stupid themselves to make the call.

If they say you're smart, they may be lying. That's what smart people do. If someone tells you you're smart, hang on to your wallet.

Colleges are the perfect example of the smart-telling strategy. Each year thousands of teenagers receive letters like this:

"You are one of the chosen few smart enough to be admitted to our college. Please send $40,000 to cover your book deposit for the first semester."

How smart are people who pay $40,000 a year to get an education that will qualify them for jobs that command a salary of $20,000 a year?

If I'm stupid, should I feel bad about it?

Absolutely not.

Being stupid shares many characteristics with being in love, primarily that you never have to say you're sorry. Also five years later, you will wonder how you ever could have been that dumb.

The friar never apologized for coming up with the brilliant idea of having Juliet pretend to be dead so Romeo would then kill himself and she would wake up and kill herself too—and neither should you.

Aren't prisons full of stupid criminals?

Half right. You'll find two kinds of popular criminals populating our prisons: the stupid and the unlucky.

Prison wardens typically divide inmates into the dangerous and the slightly less dangerous. Enlightened prison wardens divide them into smoking and nonsmoking sections.

They're all missing the point. Prisons should be divided into a stupid section and an unlucky section.

When stupid and unlucky criminals are mixed together, the smart but unlucky ones educate the stupid ones, turning them into smarter thieves. When they come out of prison, they are less stupid and, therefore, more successful crooks.

If we separated them, the stupid ones would be educated by other stupid criminals and come out even dumber than when they went in. They would be more likely to be caught when they commited their next crime, approximately an hour and a half after getting released.

Meanwhile, the smart but unlucky ones would spend their time surrounded by other unlucky criminals, which would compound the frustration of their own intelligence.

So they would be more likely to be caught when they commited their next clever crime, precisely an hour and a half after getting out of prison. When you're unlucky, the smarter the crime the better the chance you're going to get caught.

If we can't avoid stupidity, is there anything we can do to lessen the impact?

Choose your stupidity wisely.

Two hundred years ago, Benjamin Franklin, a man who flew kites in thunderstorms, advised people who complained about the government imposing taxes that "we are taxed twice as much by our idleness, three times as much by our pride, and four times as much by our folly."

Following Franklin's formula, the wise man would choose idleness over pride or folly as his preferred form of stupidity, thus dramatically decreasing his rate of taxation.

Are scientists brilliant? Or just vain enough to think they're brilliant?

"Had I been present at the Creation," King Alfonso of Spain said in the twelfth century, "I could have given the Deity some valuable advice."

So could we. Don't create kings of Spain, for example.

Alfonso was one of the first of the modern scientists, making significant advances in early astronomy when he wasn't trying to push the Moors out of Spain.

With his offer to work as a retroactive deity consultant, King

Alfonso postulated a scientific theory that would be proven popular over the next seven centuries: that because scientists come to some basic understandings of how our universe operates they can play God just as well as God can.

Actually, scientists rarely discover anything. Mostly they stumble upon something that has existed all along. Their talent for taking credit for good fortune tends to go to their heads, where they convince themselves that they have a right to do whatever it is they're capable of doing.

That's why scientists will turn a theoretical understanding of atomic interaction into atom bombs, which they engineer for the future good of the race, the insect race if not the human race.

Martin Klaproth didn't "discover" uranium. It was there all the time, happily ignored by all sorts of people who didn't need Klaproth coming along to give them good advice about new and better ways to die.

Are successful people smart or just lucky?
The exceedingly rich John Paul Getty pointed out the best way to get rich: "Rise early, work hard, strike oil."

If you follow step 3, you can skip steps 1 and 2. As a perk of being exceptionally adept at step 3, you are entitled to encourage other people to work hard while you sleep late.

We have all defied incredible odds by succeeding at life. We exist. A million-to-one shot at best.

We may make a mess of our lives, but if we last till the end of this sentence, then we have stayed alive longer than the odds say we should. While you've been reading this, millions of other life forms with as much claim to existence as you have died. Millions more never got a shot at staring at a starry starry night or eating a pint of Ben & Jerry's.

Could have been a different planet, a million different histo-
ries, several thousand different genes.

Anyone who tops a successful existence by succeeding at what
they attempt should put good luck high on their résumé. The best
fortunes are made with good fortune.

But people who succeed tend to be the kind of people who
like to take credit for their accomplishments.

They don't write many books about people who take credit
for their failures.

The successful people want you to think there's no such thing
as good luck. They already have it and don't want you to get any,
which might diminish their share.

Getting born into a family with brains, with money and connections: luck. Getting a good education, the right job, the breaks:
all luck.

The rest of us are left with lottery tickets. We keep an eye out
for that bag of money someone's got to drop in the street some-
time, somewhere, don't they?

But good luck can be cultivated, like any other talent. How?
Through inexhaustible hard work.

Which means if, unlike John Paul Getty, you have yet to
strike oil, you must get up early and work hard until you do.

Once you pass that stage, you will be able to tell everyone how
smart you were to find oil where no one else thought to look, and
you can remind yourself in your quiet moments that good luck is
a silent partner.

**Look at all the marvelous tools and conveniences we've
invented. Surely that shows our intelligence?**

We are clever, aren't we, restless inventors, ceaseless tinkerers. But
why so restless?

We wouldn't need this constant reinvention of the screw, the screwdriver, the toaster, the car, if we had got them right the first time, or even the hundredth time.

Inventors look around at the objects in their lives and think: Hmm, that doesn't work as well as it should. What if we made it better?

But if it ever did work as well as it should, they wouldn't have to make it better.

Wait a minute. Didn't we invent the airplane, the TV dinner, and cable TV?

No, we didn't. They did. The smart ones. The deviants.

We took the airplane and added bombs so we could destroy ourselves in more efficient ways than ever before.

We took the TV dinner and filled the tray with globby matter only idiots would confuse with food.

They gave us the potential for watching hundreds of TV channels. We filled those channels with mental globby matter not worth watching.

The unique features of human intelligence—genius and idiocy—exist side by side in rough harmony. The guy driving the Rolls and the guy behind the wheel of the exploding Chevy can drive through the same pothole.

The smartest people do the dumbest things because they are clever enough to attempt things that are beyond the average dummy.

But we're making progress, aren't we? We've gone from the buggy to the car?

Car crashes, air pollution, traffic jams. More successful bank robbers.

We've moved from huts to skyscrapers?

City jams, urban blight, ennui, alienation, $10 hamburgers.

Ships, airplanes, spaceships?

Without ships, we wouldn't be able to take cars from Germany, bring them to the United States, then fill the ship up with American cars and send them to Germany.

Planes enable the rich to bomb the poor without having to clean up the mess afterward.

Spaceships? Maybe, but we've gone twice as far in science fiction movies as we have in real life.

Life-saving medicine?

People can now live long enough to grow into feeble prisoners of their own age, nursing-home inmates who can't leave, hate the bad food, are shoved around by stressed-out attendants, and sedated by vegetative drugs, thus confusing the elderly with the criminally insane.

Are disasters accidents, or the result of stupidity?

The concept of human error is the great PR job of civilized man.

Every time a pilot drives a plane into the ground, a train engineer ignores signals and crashes on the wrong track, a mine operator violates safety regulations and blows the shaft—and a few hundred people who thought they were doing something else find out what Heaven is really like—we call it human error, operator mishap, pilot mistake.

We have procedures and standards, regulations and codes, that say: "Don't do that." We train them over and over again: "Don't do that." Then they go and do that.

But not to worry. That's why we have company PR experts.

We don't put morons with their minds on empty behind the wheel. If you thought we let idiots run our cockpits, why would you ever fly with us again?

It's not stupidity. That's scary. It's human error. You don't have to worry about human error because we'll put in new procedures, higher standards, stricter codes. It won't happen again—until next time.

But we have so much more than any generation before us. Isn't that a sign of our progress?

The more we have, the more failure to go around.

Everything we make is failure-based. Take any common product—this book, for example. It looks like a thousand other books you've seen, other than the title and the words.

But it probably doesn't fit in your pocket for easy transport. When you are through reading a page, you have to turn to the next one. If you're reading in bed, you have to hold it open. It may contain words or ideas you wish it didn't. It may not contain words and ideas you wish it did. It is not the perfect book. No book is.

Neither is the light that shines on the book, the chair you're sitting in, the room the chair is in, the house the room is in.

Our faults abound. What's amazing about the human race is how easily we live with our faults.

You can go through life with your pantry half stocked and get away with it. The stupid elk is quickly an ex-elk. The stupid person has friends, family, social welfare, low standards, and good luck to sustain him.

Our inventions are inspired by the faults of the inventions that went before. The new stuff we rush onto the market contains enough faults to inspire another round of inventors to design and produce more faulty merchandise.

They can make fortunes on things that never quite work right because consumers will always trade new frustrations for old.

Anytime the user's manual is more than ten pages thick, that's a sign of bad engineering. They didn't get it right inside the machine and they're counting on you to make up the difference.

But we've solved so many problems?

Within each solution is the promise of strange problems never foreseen. Take the common paper clip. Brilliant little device for holding papers together. Problem solved.

But studies show that only one out of every ten paper clips is used to hold papers together.

The other nine are lost in paper clip–shaped crevices, used to clean teeth, fingernails, and ears, and to hold ties to shirts, turned into game chips or weapons, or twisted into garbage to relieve nervous tension.

People waste money, break fillings, poke out eardrums, with a problem-solving device that was designed for none of its more popular uses.

Won't learning how stupid we are have a negative effect on us?

Bound to. So relax, settle back, and feel those IQ points melting away.

IQ points? What a waste of numbers.

Intelligence is the most overrated of human quirks because it's rated by people who have a vested interest in rating intelligence highly. It's their ace in the hole.

Tigers don't rank themselves by intelligence. But the next time you're standing within fang range of a tiger, ask yourself why, if you're so smart, he's not afraid of you.

IQ points? No one ever looked at a tiger and said, "His claws are only 97 percent as sharp as the claws on this superior tiger over here."

Points are meaningless. Any tiger is sharp enough to get the job done.

How is the stupid future shaping up?

Just because we think the human race has made a mess of this opportunity for life on a dinky planet, it doesn't mean we're pessimists.

What would it take to get us to change our idiotic ways? To stop killing one another, to clean up the air, water, and New Jersey? To switch from a misery-based system to happiness mode, in which we spent more of our lives enjoying peace, harmony, and strong beer, and less time in mess-deepening activities?

Obviously, intelligence isn't going to get the job done. It's our brains that got us into this mess in the first place.

But here's where our optimism jumps in—we're just stupid enough to stumble our way out of the mess we stumbled into.

If anything is going to see us through, it's pure dumb luck. That's one resource the human race has yet to deplete.

So how do we get out of this mess?

Got to walk that 12-step path to nirvana. While intelligence is a disease, it is curable.

Step 1: Admit who you are. I'm going to do it right now, so stand up and say it with me: "Hi, my name is Bob, and I'm an idiot."

There, don't you feel better? Unless your name's not Bob, of course.

Step 2: Repeat: "Every day in every way I'm trying to be not quite as dumb as I was the day before (which I think was a Thursday but maybe it was Tuesday)."

Steps 3–10: Don't make lists.

Step 11: Repeat step 12.

PART 3

How to Destupify:

Sixty-two Unexpected Things You Can
Do to Get Smarter, While Your Neighbor
Stays as Dumb as He Always Was

How to Destupify:
Sixty-two Unexpected Things You Can Do to Get Smarter, While Your Neighbor Stays as Dumb as He Always Was

1. Set your goals high and deep.

Even if you don't fulfill your dreams, you'll accomplish more than if you aim low. Short goals leave no room for constructive failure.

Consider these goals of remarkable people, which have little to do with common notions of success:

Scientist Albert Einstein: "I want to know how God created the world. . . . I want to know his thoughts. The rest are details."

Artist Pablo Picasso: "I'd like to live like a poor man with lots of money."

Social critic Simone de Beauvoir: "I wish that every human life might be pure, transparent freedom."

Writer Logan Smith: "For me, there is one thing that matters—to set a chime of words tinkling in the minds of a few fastidious people."

Artist Salvador Dalí: "At the age of six, I wanted to be a cook. At seven I wanted to be Napoleon. And my ambition has been growing steadily ever since."

Drummer Ringo Starr (about why he joined the Beatles): "I always wanted to play with better bands. My aim wasn't to be big and famous. It was to play with really good people."

Writer Damon Runyon: "You can keep the things of bronze and stone and give me one man to remember me just once a year."

2. Don't let the rules stop you.

Every time we think there are rules to what can and cannot be done, someone smart succeeds by completely ignoring them.

Before Ibrahim Pasha became a great eighteenth-century general, he was an observant boy in the Egyptian court, watching his father test his generals to see who was smart enough to protect the nation.

The king placed an apple in the center of a vast carpet, then challenged the generals to pick up the apple without stepping on the rug.

When none of the generals could solve the problem, the young Ibrahim asked for a chance. He walked to one side of the room, rolled the carpet up toward the middle, then reached over and picked up the apple.

3. Exploit your weaknesses.

Nearly everyone has liabilities that can lead to success as soon as you view them as assets.

"Some people have youth, some have beauty," said the old, ugly actor Edward G. Robinson. "I have menace." He turned that menace into a long career playing gangsters on the big screen.

4. Get your own cheetah.

"I just use my muscles as a conversation piece," bodybuilding movie star Arnold Schwarzenegger said, "like someone walking a cheetah down Forty-second Street."

5. If you're only half smart, be half smart twice.

Most people are not exceptional at any one thing. But they're okay at a couple of things. The trick is to find two things you're pretty good at and put them together.

"I know my limitations," cartoonist Berke Breathed said. "I

could never make it as a writer, and I could never make it as a fine artist. Thus, the world of cartooning was waiting for me to come along. I have plenty of partial ability."

6. Don't be great. Do great things.

If people do something brilliant, they get labeled as brilliant people. Don't believe your own press clippings.

In subsequent endeavors, these brilliant people may do stupid things, and frequently.

Truly great people concentrate on what they're doing, not on what they're called.

"I am not a great man," Sigmund Freud, who pioneered modern psychoanalysis, admitted. "I have made a great discovery."

7. Challenge pretensions.

Ingyo, a fifth-century Japanese emperor, was troubled by too many families filing false claims to titles of nobility. He announced a divine solution to the problem: All claimants would have to sink their arms into pots of boiling water.

The gods would protect only those with genuine claims to nobility, Ingyo explained. They alone would not be burned.

On the day of the test, only a few men showed up. Ingyo awarded them all titles without requiring immersion in the boiling water to judge their sincerity.

The unsure and the unfaithful had eliminated themselves from contention.

8. Develop an outrageous sense of confidence.

"I have no use for humility," Jackie Gleason, the TV star who styled himself the Great One, explained. "I am a fellow with an exceptional talent."

9. If you're going to be humble, also be great.

"Sometimes I amaze myself," boxing promoter Don King admitted. "I say this humbly."

"We are all worms," Winston Churchill, who guided England through World War II, admitted. "But I do believe that I am a glow-worm."

"I'm fifty-five, I'm overweight, I'm bald-headed, I'm corny," TV personality Willard Scott said, "and I'm on top of the heap."

10. Become a smarter idiot.

You only have to be smart at one thing. Just about everyone is.

People often dismiss what they're good at as being unimportant. They discount their own intelligence if it applies to something like cooking or welding. We guarantee you there are college professors out there who would give away a degree and a half if they could fix their cars without having to call in an expert.

"There is a proper dignity and proportion to be observed in the performance of every act of life," the philosopher Marcus Aurelius observed two thousand years ago. "Love the little trade which thou hast learned, and be content therewith."

Find out what you're smart at. Pursue that thread until you weave it into a rope.

11. Fake it.

Soldiers learn that if you are not naturally courageous (few people are), you can fake it by pretending to be brave.

In the heat of battle it doesn't make much difference whether your courage is authentic or well faked.

It's the same with intelligence.

Few people can tell the difference between true brains and someone acting smart. Those who can tell will be kind to those who strive.

"You gain strength, courage, and confidence by every experience in which you really stop to look fear in the face," the inspirational Eleanor Roosevelt wrote. "You are able to say to yourself, 'I lived through this horror. I can take the next thing that comes along.' . . . You must do the thing you think you cannot do."

As long as it moves you forward, it works.

12. Take a job you hate.

Working a lousy job will spur you on to do something you don't hate, and that's a step closer to something you might love, which is the intelligent way to work.

It worked for movie star Paul Newman. "I wasn't driven to acting by an inner compulsion," he admitted. "I was running away from the sporting goods business."

13. Know what you really want.

Naturalist John Muir once declared that he was richer than millionaire E. H. Harriman because "I have all the money I want and he hasn't."

14. Pray sufficiently but keep working.

Confederate general Edward Porter Alexander, one of the reasons the South almost won the Civil War, wrote this about his experiences: "It is customary to say that Providence did not intend that we should win, but I do not subscribe in the least to that doctrine. Providence did not care a row of pins about it. If it did, it was a very unintelligent Providence not to bring the business to a close—the close it wanted—in less than four years of most terrible & bloody war. . . . It was a weakness to imagine that a victory could ever come in even the slightest degree from anything except our own exertions."

15. If you can't leap, take many small steps.

You may not be able to jump up to a higher level of intelligence. But you can climb that ladder one rung at a time.

"You learn to steer your way around your own shortcomings," physicist Steven Toulmin said. "The world is made up of getting a little better at things."

16. Use the steam.

Harvey Firestone, who founded a rubber and tire company that successfully challenged the giants Goodyear and Goodrich, advised, "Nervous energy is all right if it is expended in constructive action, in doing real things. But you have to be sure that the nervous man isn't the kind that simply stirs himself and everybody around him into a turmoil. He sets the water to boiling, but he doesn't do anything with the steam."

The clever trick in any enterprise is to harness whatever steam you produce and use it to move cogs, turn wheels, go forward.

17. If you can't stop making dumb mistakes, make them faster.

Everyone screws up. But smart people don't wallow in their mistakes. They move on.

The Burpee Company ran a small mail-order poultry business in the late 1800s. They added seeds to their product line so customers could raise the food for the chickens they bought.

Few customers wanted to buy chickens through the mail. Mail-order ducks? Are you kidding? What a stupid idea. You must be an idiot.

But Atlee Burpee didn't beat himself up over his mistake. He simply switched directions and made a fortune selling seeds for flowers and vegetables, which people were happy to buy through the mail.

18. Challenge yourself the way you would a rival.

Put yourself in circumstances tough enough to force you to think your way out of them.

As science writer Robert Ardrey wrote, "We are bad-weather animals, disaster's fairest children. For the soundest of evolutionary reasons man appears at his best when times are worst."

Trust in your genes. We have the power to think better than we think we can think.

19. Restructure your time.

Look at what you do best and what you love to do the most. They should be the same thing. Count the time in a week you spend doing that. Then find ways to increase that amount of time each week. You can accumulate your intelligence quantitatively.

As Frank Deford, one of *Sports Illustrated*'s best writers, wrote, "I try never to forget that the ultimate skill is to learn what best you do, and then to try and seek to pass as much time as possible in that endeavor."

20. Take it outside.

Leave the city. Find the wilderness, what's left of it. Find some big open solitude and let your mind fill it.

Writer Edward Abbey had a wilderness explanation for the madness of poets, a kind of dark stupidity that strikes down the too intellectual.

Abbey wrote, "Our suicidal poets (Plath, Berryman, Lowell, Jarrell, et al.) spent too much of their lives inside rooms and classrooms when they should have been trudging up mountains, slogging through swamps, rowing down rivers. The indoor life is the next best thing to premature burial."

21. Make better mistakes.

Smart people make mistakes too, but not the dumb ones that mess up so many lives. We're a mistake-ingrained race. When you upgrade the level of your mistakes, you may come out looking clever.

Pianist Josef Hofmann found himself in a dumb situation at a concert. With the orchestra waiting for him to start, he turned to a woman in the front row and asked to see her program.

"I forget what comes first," he explained.

Another musician seeking to avoid embarrassment would have sat there fretting his brain to remember the first piece.

Hofmann solved his slipup in a direct, ingenious way. Instead of being humiliated by his mistake, he became a musical legend.

22. Try strange connections.

Peanut butter and chocolate? Who would have guessed it until someone tried it and made a tasty fortune?

Jokes often make us laugh by connecting the ordinarily unconnectable.

"Waiter, what's that fly doing in my soup?"

"I think it's the backstroke."

Swimming in soup. Absurd. But a successful, if old, joke.

"Nonsense and beauty have close connections," the writer E. M. Forster remarked, contradicting common sense to find an uncommon sense.

Or as the master of nonsense, Lewis Carroll, wrote in *Through the Looking Glass:* "Sometimes I've believed as many as six impossible things before breakfast."

That's how to get an early start on everyone else. Wild connections can lead to poetry, romance, or the Pet Rock fortune.

23. Give up.

Don't fight it. Cut loose. Drift, daydream.

All the best artists and writers do.

Consider poet Emily Dickinson's clear advice: "To make a prairie it takes a clover and one bee, one clover and a bee, and revery. The revery alone will do, if bees are few."

Creative thinkers unfocus from their problems. They let their minds wander until the subconscious makes itself heard. The answer comes like a dream, almost unearned, always valuable.

24. Ask someone smarter than you are what to do.

If you can't solve a problem, perhaps Socrates or da Vinci or Einstein could. They're not available? No problem.

Curl up in a cozy room by yourself. Read their writings. Close your eyes, ask them your question, and listen to what comes into your mind.

That's Socrates talking. You say it's not? Then who is it? Just you talking to yourself? Well, that's a start, the basic trick that writers use.

Have you ever had a dream where some famous person appeared? That was you too, and yet it was also them.

"To know is nothing at all," the wise writer Anatole France said. "To imagine is everything."

25. Shoot the brave ones.

During the Civil War a Confederate general ordered his men not to fire at a particular Union officer because he showed such courage on the field of battle.

Later, Gen. Stonewall Jackson explained the error of this strategy: "Shoot the brave officers," Jackson commanded. "The cowards will run away and take their men with them."

26. Test for idiocy.

When confronted with Robert Browning's poem *Sordellow*, the writer Douglas Jerrold could not follow it and confessed, "I am an idiot."

When his wife read the poem, she declared it gibberish. "Thank God," Jerrold replied, "I am not an idiot."

27. Violate proverbs.

When Lyndon Johnson was the majority leader of the Senate, he pushed the other senators into long, overtime sessions. "What's all the hurry," one of them asked. "Rome wasn't built in a day."

"No," a fellow senator replied, "but Lyndon Johnson wasn't foreman on that job."

28. If you can't sell it, give it away.

When painter Joszi Koppay couldn't get a commission from the wealthy publisher Adolph Ochs to paint a portrait of Ochs's daughter, Iphigene, Koppay offered to do the painting for free.

Along with the finished portrait, Koppay sent a bill for $1,000. Ochs reminded the artist that he had agreed to paint Iphigene for free.

"Your daughter has such a beautiful face, it was a joy to paint it," Koppay explained. "But the body was dull and bored me. It is for this that I charge you $1,000."

29. Fool your rage.

Anger blocks intelligence. Strong anger obliterates otherwise sensible intentions.

A member of President Lincoln's cabinet was having trouble with a subordinate. Lincoln suggested that he write the troublemaker a nasty letter expressing his rage.

When the cabinet officer had written the letter, Lincoln further advised him, "You don't want to send that letter. Put it in the stove. It's a good letter and you had a good time writing it and feel better. Now burn it and write another."

30. Switch hit.

Train yourself to be ambidextrous. Leonardo da Vinci could draw with one hand while writing with the other. President James Garfield wrote Greek with one hand while writing Latin with the other. Switch-hitting baseball players cut down the pitcher's advantage.

The effort involved with teaching yourself to go left if you always go right is a difficult and, therefore, liberating experience. Liberation smartens.

31. Develop the portion of the brain labeled ESP.

People of rational intelligence claim ESP does not exist, while others think they've been using it productively for years.

The thirteenth-century monk Roger Bacon left writings that accurately predicted automobiles, airplanes, modern ships, gunpowder, bombs, the telescope, and the microscope—hundreds of years before the technology to develop such machines was conceived.

32. Work outside time.

We rush around by the minute, charge by the quarter hour, rely on nanosecond technology, as if that timing was truly important to a life intelligently lived.

Devotion to time is a trap that dulls the mind, like the obsession with money. Artists cannot approach inspiration until they stare off into space, not into time.

How important are those seconds and minutes by which we monitor our lives? Clocks didn't even have minute hands until 1687. The hour hands were sufficient because no one had to be any more accurate than that.

If you hear that ticking, it's not just the clock but your life that's ticking away. The trick is not to listen to the tick.

33. Find a sacred cow and bet against it.

Holding something sacred exposes a weakness. But because it's considered sacred, most people are reluctant to take advantage of it.

Not the ancient Persian king Cambyses II. He broke the siege of the Egyptian city of Memphis in the sixth century B.C. when he discovered that the Egyptian defenders held the cat to be sacred.

Cambyses simply had his soldiers gather up all the stray cats they could find in the surrounding villages and throw them over the city walls.

Horrified at such heresy but powerless to stop it, the Egyptians ended the sacrilege the only way they could: They surrendered.

34. Move to a stupid state.

If you move from California or New York to Arizona or Arkansas, your IQ will automatically go up 50 points.

Or move to a college town, where brains aren't something you get punished for.

As the actor Wally Cox lamented, "When I was a kid in the Midwest I got straight A's in school, and I spent thirteen years on the psychiatrist's couch paying for it."

35. Evaluate your talents accurately.

It's incorrect to discount your abilities. It's not ego if you're right.

"I'm young, I'm fast, I'm pretty," Muhammad Ali said during his undefeated years, "and I can't possibly be beat."

Ali was often put down for bragging. But he was rarely put down inside the ring. Not only was he correct about his talents, but he advanced the art of outmouthing your opponent to get a psychological edge (and pump up gate receipts).

36. Steal from the best.

You don't always need creative ideas if you know how to steal from creative people. As Dale Carnegie, the inspirational author, admitted, "The ideas I stand for are not mine. I borrowed them from Socrates. I swiped them from Chesterfield. I stole them from Jesus. And I put them in a book."

37. Develop a strong inner drive.

People who are intrinsically motivated push deeper than people who are motivated by the rewards and punishments imposed by society or authorities.

As a child Blaise Pascal locked himself inside his room for several days and refused to come out. When his parents finally got him to open the door, the young Pascal, who was to become a brilliant mathematician, had figured out all of Euclid's geometrical propositions on his own.

38. Don't stop.

Losers might become winners if they didn't quit early. Inner greatness takes commitment, more than most people think appropriate.

Hokusai, the eighteenth-century Japanese painter whose work influenced the Impressionist movement in Europe, painted all his life. On his deathbed at eighty-nine, he said, "If heaven had granted me five more years, I could have become a real painter."

That's the kind of effort we're talking about. Too much? Do you have something better to do with your life?

Persistence requires that you go on after you think you've been persistent. It worked for Albert Einstein.

"I think and think for months and years," he said. "Ninety-nine times the conclusion is false. The hundredth time I am right."

39. Do what you haven't done before.

You're already smart enough to do what you know how to do. To get smarter, take on new challenges.

This takes courage, which comes from effort. How do soldiers find the courage to carry on against certain death? They fall back on training. They do what they were taught to do. They don't overthink. They charge.

If soldiers can find fortitude under such daunting conditions, you can find the courage to take risks in ordinary life.

If you don't try something difficult, you will fail by default. It's smarter to fail by daring. Fail going forward so you learn something that may make the next charge successful. But keep something in reserve. Failure can sap energy. Save enough firepower to start over again.

40. Study outside your main field of endeavor.
The great English scientist Isaac Newton was known for his work in physics and the promotion of scientific experimentation at a time when the scientific method was not an accepted course of action.

Newton was also a secret student of more arcane studies. After his death, it was found that he'd written extensively on the occult, astrology, and alchemy.

41. Develop a backup plan in case your first brainstorm doesn't play out.
Siam's king Prajadhipok bought a revolution insurance policy in 1935. When he was usurped while on a visit to England, he simply stayed in Britain, living lavishly on his unique form of unemployment compensation.

42. Identify the real competition.
Ballet star Mikhail Baryshnikov was driven to greatness by trying to match the toughest competition of all.

"I do not try to dance better than anyone else," he said. "I only try to dance better than myself."

43. Sharpen your critical judgment without having to intellectualize your reactions.
Movie mogul Harry Cohn knew exactly how to tell if a film was any good. "If my fanny squirms, it's bad. If my fanny doesn't squirm, it's good."

44. Make your weaknesses flamboyant.

"I don't remember anybody's name," said Zsa Zsa Gabor, a woman who became famous for being famous. Instead of letting her shortcoming embarrass her, she turned forgetfulness into an essential flair.

"Why do you think the 'dahling' thing started?" she explained.

45. Keep a dream journal.

When you go to bed, set a notebook and pen on the night table and tell yourself that when you wake from a dream you will write it down.

Record everything you remember from the dream and any thoughts you may have about it.

Repeat for twenty-one nights.

On the twenty-second night, before you go to sleep, ask yourself a question about a problem that's been occupying your mind. Ask for a solution to come in your dream. Even if it doesn't, something interesting will.

Your subconscious mind knows many things that you don't know consciously. Once your subconscious realizes that you're listening through the dream journal, it will flood you with information (dreams, daydreams, inspirations) that you didn't have before.

46. Ask too many questions.

As they used to say in the Chicago newspaper racket, "If your mother says she loves you, check it out."

Or as Ann Landers put it, "Don't accept your dog's admiration as conclusive evidence that you are wonderful."

47. If you can't convince yourself, convince others.

Most intelligent people appear to know what they're doing. But you don't have to know what you're doing as long as people think you know what you're doing. If civilization teaches us anything, it's to keep up appearances.

The great filmmaker John Huston drew story boards for every scene of his masterpiece, *The Maltese Falcon*, which he directed early in his career.

He didn't draw the story boards because he needed them to visualize scenes before he started shooting. He drew them because he thought the people working with him thought he needed them.

"I didn't want to lose face with the crew," Huston explained. "I wanted to give the impression that I knew what I was doing." He's given that impression to anyone who's ever seen the movie.

48. Flex your brain.

When you find yourself thinking there's only one way to do something, that's a sure sign that there's another, and probably better, way to get the job done.

"I am a man of fixed and unbending principles," the politician Everett Dirksen claimed, "the first of which is to be flexible at all times."

49. Free yourself from outside expectations.

Don't expect much from society. Relying upon the system makes you soft. Intelligence is a hard thing.

If you get your priorities straight, it simplifies matters and leaves you time to think.

The Irish writer Brendan Behan had his priorities clearly in line. "I respect kindness to human beings first of all, and kindness to animals. I don't respect the law. I have total irreverence for anything connected with society, except that which makes the roads safer, the beer stronger, the food cheaper, and old men and old women warmer in the winter and happier in the summer."

50. Help your enemies outsmart themselves.

Florida police set up a clever trap. They put up a sign on a highway frequented by drug runners that said: "Narcotics Inspection Ahead."

Then they hid by the sign. Anytime a car made a sudden U-turn, they stopped it and searched for drugs.

51. Learn how to learn from criticism.

General John "Blackjack" Pershing, one of the toughest leaders of World War I, expected as much from himself as from others.

As Gen. George Marshall, who served under Pershing in that war, commented, "He could listen to severe criticisms, just as though it was about a man in another country."

52. Fool yourself first.

When Theodore Roosevelt was a boy, he suffered from severe asthma and other crippling problems. "There were all kinds of things of which I was afraid at first," he said. "But by acting as if I were not afraid, I gradually ceased to be afraid."

Later in life Roosevelt was the most active man anyone knew. Although he loved to hunt, even African safaris did not offer enough engagement for his restless mind. So he took a hundred books along with him. Every moment he wasn't hunting, he was reading.

53. Focus on the deeper goals.

Writer Sherwood Anderson put goals in perspective. "Try to be humble," he advised. "Smartness kills everything. . . . The object of art is not to make salable pictures. It's to save yourself."

54. Look for paradoxes.

Self-canceling ideas can open your mind instead of shutting it down.

As philosopher Daniel Dennett said, "There is a good strategy to adopt whenever there is a stagnation in science: Find the thing that everybody agrees on; deny that and you probably break through the self-evident truth that turns out to be false, however self-evident. One should always look for paradoxes, because they tend to be breakthroughs."

55. Don't give up at quitting time.

It's easy to give up. When the going gets tough, the reasonable try again. But after a few failures, they usually move on.

Poncélet, a French mathematician, was forced to fight in Napoleon's army in the disastrous invasion of Russia. Captured by the Russians, he was locked in a prison for two years.

Without paper or writing instruments, Jean Poncélet put his imprisonment to use, solving math problems. He scratched formulas on the walls of his cell with pebbles, solving all the axioms of projective geometry.

If he could do that, what can we do if we don't give up?

56. Break the TV habit.

TV is a habit-forming drug, ruining more minds than marijuana or heroin. According to the Annenberg Public Policy Center, kids spend an average of $4\frac{1}{2}$ hours watching TV every day. That's 1,642 hours a year or 642 more hours than they spend in school.

TV shows demand disconcentration. TV teaches the dismissal of focus, disengagement from the thinking process, and a reliance on easy answers to misstated problems.

TV shows are so simpleminded, they reward our not paying attention. We almost always do something else while we watch their shows: eat, fold the laundry, balance the checkbook, do homework.

Then we carry that skill of vague focus into other parts of our life, where sharp focus is required.

Modern cars are built like TV systems: comfortable chair, no outside noises, easy to drift. How many car accidents occur because people are paying only vague attention to their driving?

Focus doesn't mean nervous attention. Focus requires relaxed concentration on the matter at hand, the way a great shortstop fields his position. They don't teach that in school. They should.

57. Show confidence in your doubts.

Field Marshal Bernard Montgomery, who led Britain's military, was speaking of the quality of great leaders when he said, "He must radiate confidence, even when he himself is not too certain of the outcome."

That quality applies also to intelligence. Uncertainty is a component of most rational analysis. To turn halting analysis into successful action, confidence in a dubious outcome is required, and is often sufficient unto itself.

58. Improve your reading.

Everything you need to know is available in books. Some of the finest minds educated themselves by reading their way through the public library.

But some 36 million American adults read below the eighth-grade level, leaving their minds to starve when a wealth of intelligence is set before them.

59. Slip by authoritarian roadblocks.

You don't have to agree with authorities. They're only authorities because the people who quote authorities need someone to quote.

As the high-tech entrepreneurial maverick Guy Kawasaki writes, "If a person with the right credentials says something can be done, then it probably can be done. If the person says it can't be done, then probably it still can be done."

If you think it can be done, then find a way to do it.

60. Learn plumbing.

John Gardner, former secretary of the Department of Health, Education and Welfare, put the skill of thinking in perspective: "The society which scorns excellence in plumbing because plumbing is a humble activity, and tolerates shoddiness in philosophy because philosophy is an exalted activity, will have neither good plumbing nor good philosophy. Neither its pipes nor its theories will hold water."

Find something you do well, then practice until you do it better. You will strengthen your skill, which fosters intelligence.

After you have learned plumbing, learn carpentry. Stop when you have run out of things to learn.

61. Read poetry.

Poems will stimulate your thinking in ways that nothing else can. There are hundreds of inspirational poets out there who can stir your mind. Keep reading till you find them.

Consider this from poet and physician William Carlos Williams: "It is difficult to get the news from poems. Yet men die miserably every day for lack of what is found there."

Or as practical philosopher Daniel Dennett said, "If you want to remember something, it's useful to make a rhyme out of it. . . . Maybe it's better still to turn it into a song, because songs stick in the memory in a way that mere spoken words don't. Poetry sticks much more readily than prose."

62. Watch whom you kiss.

No matter how dumb you feel at times, you will never seem quite so stupid if you just remember one thing: Never kiss a rattlesnake on the mouth.